COURAGE AND GRACE

From Broken to Blissful

The Journey of Building Joy
During Your Recovery from Abuse

Susan Ball

Library and Archives Canada Cataloguing in Publication

Ball, Susan Lillian, author

    Courage and grace: from broken to blissful, the journey of building joy during your recovery from abuse / Susan Lillian Ball. -- Canada-Uk edition.

Includes bibliographical references.
Issued in print and electronic formats.
ISBN 978-0-9940257-9-1 (softcover).--

    1. Abused wives--Rehabilitation. 2. Marital violence--Psychological aspects. I. Title.

HV6626.B26   2017 362.82'92   C2016-907778-0

                                            C2016-907779-9

Copyright 2017© Susan Ball

Published by: Survive It Press
Suite Bee, 804 Byron Street South
Whitby, ON, L1N 4R8, Canada

No parts of this publication may be reproduced, stored in a retrieval system, or transmitted in any form or by any means, electronic, mechanical, photocopying, recording, or otherwise, without the prior written permission of the copyright owner. Some names and identifying details have been changed to protect the privacy of individuals.

It should be noted that readers are likely to see results once they finish the book and consistently apply the instructions mentioned within it. Nonetheless, the book is a compilation of the author's experiences and successes that has particularly worked for her. The author and publisher do not warrant or represent that the readers will see the desired results and hereby disclaim any liability or harm resulting from the reader's reliance on the material within this book.

The author and publisher have made every effort to keep the information within the book as accurate and reliable as possible, however, the publisher and author do not make any representations or warranties, express or implied, about the completeness, accuracy, reliability, suitability or availability with respect to the information and/or guidance provided within the book.

The author of this book authorises buyers of *Courage and Grace* to copy the exercises without limits for personal use and continued recovery. For more resources or extended permissions, go to: www.susanball.ca

Author: Susan Ball, susanball.ca
Editor: Sheryl Wright, sherylwright.com
Cover Design: Sarah Lever, www.montouk.com
Cover Photography: Miguel Hortiguela, photographybymiguel.com

Survive It Press is an imprint of FORT MAY Corp

Early Praise for Courage and Grace

"Susan Ball shares her own profound journey with her readers through compassion and love, as only a triumphant woman can - having walked the walk of abuse. Both women and men who have a sense that there must be something more for them than living in abusive relationships, find hope in the support and guidance which is now available to them in Susan's book and companion workbook. *Courage and Grace* offers clear and tangible advice and self-awareness exercises on how to build their inner strength and identify a higher purpose to gain the incentive to release the hold abuse has had on their lives. This book is a true gift to anyone looking to embark on the journey of courage and living in grace outside abuse."

>Linda Berger, Women's Empowerment and Transformation Expert
>linda@coachlindaberger.com

"What we've always respected about Susan Ball is that she's a strong, smart voice for empowered women everywhere. Since she's walked the path herself, she's also an informed voice. There's no better mentor anywhere for women who've experienced pain in their personal lives and choose to emerge victoriously."

>Scot and Emily McKay
>X & Y Communications
>www.scotandemily.com/podcast

I was captivated by this incredible, eloquently written book from page 1! Susan Ball gives a very confronting insight into the world of domestic violence, and yet it is fuelled with so much Courage and Grace. Susan tells her own story so powerfully while offering enormous hope, inspiration, and practical tools (including a workbook) for anyone ready to escape the horror of domestic violence. If that is you then this book is a must, I highly recommend it.

>Jane Whiting, Relationship Coach
>Quantum Coaching with Jane
>janewhiting.com

Courage and Grace by Susan Ball has a singular focus: to empower women through their own personal story. Yet, what makes *Courage and Grace* impactful is that Susan disallows any victimization to be a part of the solution. While Susan shares her own story--including when she was stuck in her own victim mentality--but where Susan lingers is in the energy of what's possible. If you are reading this and you feel stuck in a relationship that is abusive, buy a copy of *Courage and Grace* before night fall. While reading, Susan provides opportunities for readers to pause and reflect by using the Workbook exercises; do every one of these guided, insightful activities. Susan writes with honesty about the very, real fears she faced ("Courage to Escape" and "Break the Cycle") and offers her readers practical, specific steps to take to live in the energy of courage and grace.

>Anella Wetter, M. Ed., RYT
>Writer & Speaker, Empowerment & Relationship Coach
>www.anellawetter.com

Dedication

Dedicated with love to the one extraordinary and kind person who stood beside me while I grew, healed and let go, and helped me unravel the horror through love, support, and guidance. You know who you are.

Foreword

by Elizabeth Payea-Butler

When Susan Ball asked me to write the foreword to her new book, I was amazed, amused, and very surprised. I hadn't talked to Susan for a while but had been watching her journey on Facebook. When I thought back to our time together, it began when we were children, and the fascinating part about that was Susan, and I got along quite well. We both enjoyed each other's company, and I even remember a vacation that we went to at Wasaga Beach. Through the years, Susan grew and developed, and we grew apart, simply because our families didn't meet up as often. I don't think we knew what each other was doing, or what each of us might have been experiencing.

Many years later, but only a few years ago, I bumped into Susan, and we decided to have coffee. Now, I love having coffee chats and getting caught up, and Susan had so much to tell me, which you too will discover. I say, "had," because truly, at that time in her life, she *had* to tell me everything. I listened patiently, and I listened patiently, and I did offer some advice. Now, I did know then that, Susan was not open to the advice I gave her. However, she was good enough to continue to listen to what I had to say.

We probably, over the next month or so, only met up a few times, and Susan even took a class I was facilitating. Yes, her stubborn nature showed up and her determination to stay stuck where she was. But, she began to soften, and I guess I was lucky because I was able to shake the tree finally. After that, I once again lost track of where she went, and it turned out that she and her new husband moved to the East Coast, and set up in a small community there. Through the amazing world of Facebook, we can stay connected to all the people we care about. I was able to see there, those things she started, and things she stopped, and things she started, and things she stopped. Then, Susan began to travel and take journeys, and experience things in a way only travelling can provide. She began learning about other people and experiencing a much bigger world than the small homes we inhabit.

When I saw she was writing a blog, I was so impressed. She began to do things that I could follow easily on Facebook. I noticed she was writing articles, and I noticed she was blogging, and then I noticed she was starting to do some counselling to help other women, who had, or were now going through experiences she had survived. In turn, she utilised her experiences, bringing together all her resources, and is absolutely skilled at assisting other women determined to escape any situation they no longer want to find themselves in.

This book is a foundation piece for any woman, who is experiencing abuse, fear, or is stuck in a place they don't want to be. I'm highly recommending that you simply read the book without any judgment, and utilise the resources that are available to you. I'm incredibly amazed and amused, and no longer surprised, but am very proud that Susan took the time to write her story and make it useful to help others. Congratulations, Susan.

Elizabeth Payea-Butler – www.EGBCoaching.com

Why You Need to Read This Book

SURVIVING IS NOT THRIVING!

This book is for the woman who is ready, no eager, to break the chains of victim'hood and actually move on with her life. It is for those who want to rebel against the system and put themselves front and centre in their story.

If you have experienced domestic violence, I want to support and encourage you along the path from fear to courage, and from misery to bliss. No woman belongs in an abusive relationship. Never, ever! If you have been waiting for someone to help you, don't worry, this book provides many of the answers you need. I'll share my experience, failures, and in time success, and I'll help you find your triumph too.

If you doubt your decision to leave, believing that if you give it one more try, he might change, or you're clinging to and living the victim's life and being told to be satisfied in your role as a survivor, I'm here to tell you otherwise. I've been there, and I know better. You were once a thriving, vivacious woman, before you were manipulated and abused. If you're ready to rediscover the woman, you once were or dream you can be, pull on your big-girl panties because I'm about to hand you your *Get-Out-of-Jail-Free* card. Yes! Remember, in this life, your safety and dreams are not a game for someone else to play with. Neither are your children.

In this book and the companion workbook, I take you step-by-step in recognising, addressing, and overcoming all the hurdles your abuser has placed before you. I'll show you how to get help, how to help yourself, and how to help your kids. And together, we will identify and target those limiting beliefs that led you to an abuser and kept you trapped in the cycle of violence and the victim'hood.

Finally, I'll give you the tools and insights to help you learn to love and respect yourself and create the life you and your kids deserve. I want you to be free, confident, and proactive in writing your next chapter. There may be difficult moments, but you won't be afraid to face your deepest emotional fears. It's time to close the last chapter and fearlessly open a new one.

I will warn you now, this book is not for you if you like being a victim or enjoy the false status society grants those we label victims. If you intend to hold onto your victim story for dear life, this book will not suit you nor will you find it soothing. My soul purpose is to give you the direction and tools you need to break free of victim'hood, and awaken your life's potential, to find your courage and your grace.

Follow me Blissful Thrivers, and we'll get started...

Contents

Forward by Elizabeth Payea-Butler 7
Why You Need to Read This Book 10
    Surviving is Not Thriving! 10
Introduction 17
    You Are Not Alone 17
    The Victim Story 21
    This Is Why I Do What I Do! 22
Chapter One 25
    Finding Your Courage 25
    Courage to Escape 30
    Darkness Into Light 32
    Kick Your Mind into Solution Mode 38
Chapter Two 41
    Moving with Grace from Broken to Blissful 41

Getting Unstuck Starts Here 44
Who Are You Blaming? 45
The Broken to Blissful Method 47
Free Your Voice... 49
Our Conscious Brain Voice.. 50
Our Gut Voice 51
Gut versus Ego 52
What is My Exciting, Juicy, Heart-Centered Goal?...... 56
Adopting Grace 57
Gratitude 58
Release 60
Authenticity... 62
Find Your Authentic Self 63
Getting Your Life in Gear 67
Survivor versus Blissful Thrivers 68
Embracing Your Blissful Thriver 71
Sensational & Vivid Visualisation 72
Triggers 77
On Your Journey You Need to Celebrate 79

Chapter Three 87
How to Avoid Recapture.. 87
The Three Myths 91
What is Love?... 96
Why Making Him Happy Doesn't Bring Happiness 98
Rebel Self-Love 100
What You Reflect, You Attract 102

- Launch Your Greatest Love Affair............................ 105
- Nurture Your Self-Love 112
- Our Children 122
- Break the Cycle 124
- Custody, Visitation, and The Courts 126
- His New Special Friend 128

Chapter Four 135
- Moving Out of the Victim'Hood 135
- Banish Your Lies 139
- Anticipatory Fear 142
- Activate and Embrace Your Blissful Thriver 145
- The Anatomy of a Limiting Belief 153
- Turning Limiting Beliefs into Validating Beliefs........ 155
- Taking Action... 159
- Writing Your Dream Life... 164

Resources 166

Appendix A..167
- Broken to Blissful Foundational Toolkit.................... 167
- Getting Started with Writing Prompts....................... 170
- Name IT! 171
- Rage and Weep Exercise 173
- Breathing Exercises 176
- Disconnecting and Reconnecting................................ 178
- Writing from the Heart..180

Appendix B... 183
- The 7 Warning Signs of a Mean-Spirited Dick 183

Appendix C 189
    Breathing Exercises and Self-Guided Meditation 189
Last Thoughts... 190
    How to Contact Susan 191

Introduction

YOU ARE NOT ALONE

Interestingly, the catalyst for my transformation into a Self-Love Activist & Women's Freedom Coach began with a passionate whirlwind romance. I was a broke single mom living in a 3-story walk-up. One Saturday night, I scraped together a bit of money to go out with a friend. What a treat. Getting dressed up and going out to dance, laugh, chat and have some fun.

I noticed someone was staring at me from the bar. Honestly, the attention was welcome. Eye contact led to a dance which led to an evening of laughing and talking. I felt beautiful and wanted. I felt my troubles and worries melting away. We had only been dating for a couple of weeks when he started pushing to move in together. He would help with the girls and support me financially. Ease my burdens and make my life a little easier. He was handsome, rugged, and passionate. I was losing myself in the dream he was offering, and it felt so good.

I was swept off my feet and fell deeply madly in love.

He purchased a dream house with a large backyard for my beautiful daughters and me. The house was located two hours away from my family and friends. I didn't drive and was concerned about being so far away from "home." He assured me that he would drive me to visit anyone, anytime I desired. It wasn't long after moving into the house when he insisted on getting married, and as soon as possible. "Why not," I said and donned a gown and said my vows.

The very first morning of our married life together he reached to take my hand. We were on our way to Niagara Falls for our honeymoon. I expected this was going to be one of the happiest days of my life. But something was different. He squeezed my hand very hard and said, "Now that you are my wife, you will do as you're told, how you're told, and when you're told."

"You are what you attract."
Susan Ball

For longer than I should have, I tried to believe the dream he sold me. I wondered if perhaps it was my fault; that I should have seen it coming but didn't because I'd been convinced I was stupid. But I was stronger than I expected.

In a series of small, scary steps, I left.

Like many of you, the removal of my physical self from the toxicity of an abusive relationship felt, at the time, like the biggest step I'd make. But it wasn't. In fact, it was the smallest and easiest step. Finding, encouraging and embracing joy again, that was the hardest step.

My purpose now is to guide you to step up to the next level of your being; to motivate you from victim and survivor to a thriving woman, living a vibrant and fulfilling life.

For me, my world shifted when I realised it was time for change within myself. I'd successfully removed myself and my daughters from a physically harmful situation, but I continued to carry the trauma within myself. I was done with pitying myself and playing the victim. Even though I'd been through the fires of an abusive relationship, I decided not to allow that toxicity to define my future. I was ready to let go of my victim story and begin to create my fearless, vibrant, success story.

But... I didn't know how!

I went to group therapy, and the conversations were about how we had been abused, and who got it worse. We were revelling in our victim story and patting each other on the back for being a victim.

I remember at one session in particular, we were handed a piece of paper, listing the ten characteristics of your abuser. The common ones included: isolation, volatile mood swings, and blaming you for everything. We were asked to choose which of these traits were present in our relationship with our personal abusers, and I could tick them all off.

It is easy to search the internet for numerous checklists for abusive behaviour too. But these are hindsight exercises and do nothing to heal your heartbreak and encourage you to create a life you love. They simply keep you attached to your abuser.

What I eventually learned, and what should be taught to all people entering the dating phase, is how to spot the true signs of an abuser before it's too late. I've created my own, the 7 Signs of a Mean-Spirited Dick. I invite you to share them freely with all the women you know, especially anyone just entering the dating world. You can find them in Appendix B.

Let's not get ahead of ourselves. There is a great deal of healing, growing, and creating that needs to take place before seeking out a new relationship. The tools and resources I'm sharing have been developed to move you from seeing yourself as less than to loving yourself as a whole and valuable individual.

I want you to approach your life and any new relationships from the place of wholeness. Once you feel whole, you will ask what value does someone else add to your life. You won't look for someone to complete you or your life. You will know you are complete and that your life is full and rich. You are your best friend, dinner date, and have no issue buying yourself flowers!

You are a Blissful Thriver.

The Victim Story

Not once in any of the six or seven group meetings I attended, did we talk about goals, self-love, healthy relationships, letting go, or healing. We simply talked about our victim-ness.

I felt stuck in a mess of my own negative labels and limiting beliefs. I knew the real me was hiding deep down under the pile of labels I'd acquired. I just had to uncover me again. I longed for the me that was free and confident and felt equipped to tackle anything she set her mind to. I missed me! I wanted to find me again and live my dream life. I wanted to be me, the real me, the one I had lost in the victim'hood.

I began to write new chapters in my story.

I learned the first and best way to move on is to start by loving yourself again. Quite honestly, once I learned some strategies to get past my self-judgement and let go of all the negative beliefs and labels, the opportunities to create big, bold, fearless new chapters were endless!

This Is Why I Do What I Do!

Sharing my story and the tools I have discovered, enjoyed and learned from, is the reason why I do what I do. I want to reach out to women and encourage them to free their voice and shine brightly in their personal light.

Courage and Grace is a reflection of my own healing journey, and it will guide and support your transition from Broken to Blissful.

To begin, I have created a complete set of Foundational Toolkit for you. Each is designed to address the past, honour your feelings of loss and anger, and connect with the true you, the person you know you are, deep-down in your very soul.

My Foundational Toolkit can be found in Appendix A

The companion *Courage and Grace Workbook* will guide you in your healing journey. The Workbook is filled with exercises and guidance designed to move you from the place of feeling Broken to an empowered, healed, woman who embraces the Blissful life she has created for herself.

The tools and exercises will help you rebuild, forgive, set achievable badass goals and build on your everyday successes and each moment of joy. Each is designed to be focused on the future with a brief glance at your past as a learning tool.

Some of the questions will be tough. I won't lie. In your recovery journey exploring the tough questions is where you can discover your passions and dreams. And that's where you begin to move and step into your future with excitement and determination. Most importantly, I want you to know that you are not alone in your recovery. I've been there, and I've learned valuable lessons which helped me create a fabulous new adventure.

Sharing them with you and helping you recover and capture joy and happiness, is my greatest gift.

Tapping into your true potential is no idle endeavour. It demands creativity, dedication, and a whole lot of hustle.

You've got a whole bunch of outdated rules that determine what you do, don't do, should do, and shouldn't do. These rules limit your thinking and limit your behaviour. Let's tear up your boring, outdated rule book and set you free.

Give yourself permission to be brutally honest with yourself. It takes courage to be completely vulnerable. We can only change what we acknowledge. Being honest will lead you to the gift of living a big, bold, blissful life filled with love, laughter, and joy.

Enough chit-chat, let's get started.

Courage and Grace

Chapter One

"The only thing that is ultimately real about your journey is the step that you are taking at this moment."
Eckhart Tolle

FINDING YOUR COURAGE

The Breaking Point

I ran to the police station, my head still reeling from being choked to blacking-out but I knew I had to make him stop. I ran and ran and screamed as I got closer to the station. He was hot on my heels running after me, threatening to kill me, and I knew if I didn't get inside the police station I would die.

My screams caught the attention of an officer just getting out of her cruiser, and she ran to meet me to bring me inside the station. She radioed for the door to be opened. "Assailant in pursuit!" I actually believed he would stop when he saw the police, but he didn't. He kept coming and was getting closer, and I started screaming. She held me closer and got me inside where I was handed over to another nice officer.

At that precise moment, my abuser hit the door of the station, and he verbally threatened the officer and then reached out to punch her. The other officers stormed him, put him in cuffs, and took him downstairs to the jail cells.

I sat in the little interview room, and they just let me cry and cry. An officer brought me a coffee then said my abuser had been charged with assault and uttering death threats.

I was safe!

There was a barrage of photos of the big red marks on my throat. You could see each of his finger marks clearly on my neck. They took pictures of my back where he dragged me. Pictures, just lots of pictures. The police were so gentle and kind. Never pushed me or rushed me.

The really creepy part… the whole time I could hear my abuser shouting and cursing and threatening me from the cells. I would shake when I heard his voice and the police would reassure me he couldn't get out but there was something about his blood-curdling screams that unnerved me.

They saw my angst and distress and sent an officer down to monitor the cells so they could turn off the sound.

Peace. Quiet…

I was escorted home, and the officer went all around the house securing windows and doors for me. Then he told me that my abuser would be out on bail by morning, but he would have a restraining order on him and if he showed up anywhere near the property to call right away. I went to my girls' room and laid down with my youngest and slept. When I woke up my throat was so swollen I could hardly speak, and my kids were horrified to see the bruises around my neck. I knew I had to leave town and start over again. I knew this was not the way to raise two wee girls. I knew it was not the way I wanted to be treated. I knew it was time to move on.

The plan came together over the course of two weeks, and during that time, he would park his car just outside the range of the restraining order, stand near the hood and stare at the house. Going outside was scary. I pulled the girls out of school, and we just stayed indoors. I would sneak to my neighbours who would do a little shopping for me, so we had food. They would sneak it in through the back window. Time to go was getting closer, and although my heart was breaking and I didn't have two cents to call my own, I knew it was the right thing to do.

No excuses. My children and I deserved better. Period.

My last night cuddling my two little girls was magical. We sat on the couch all warm and cosy and read their favourite book *The Lion, The Witch, and The Wardrobe*. Both of them vowed to stay up all night so they wouldn't miss a minute of the story. Of course, they fell asleep, and I sat in the quiet, dark thinking about how we would be uprooted from our home tomorrow. <u>All because I married the wrong person.</u> Simply because I made a decision that hurt all of us deeply. This was happening! I had to be strong because I wanted more for them than to see their mother as a victim of domestic abuse. I wanted them to know that abuse was not right or normal or to be tolerated at any time in their lives. So I sat in the dark with one small child on each side and knew that I was making the right choice. I had to rip the bandage off so we could heal.

The tears flowed because I could remember the dream and how desperately I wanted the life he promised us. I was also pissed that he had given and then taken it away without even a second thought to how we would all be hurt.

How dare he?

And to top it all off, I found out, through the police about his affair. Imagine my humiliation to have a cop stand at my door asking me why I had bailed him out of jail and me looking shocked and saying, "I did no such thing." Right at the same moment, me and the cop realised the woman who bailed him out was, in fact, the Other Woman. Yeah okay. Now I feel like a complete idiot. The officer was so kind, he offered to come in and chat. I let him, recognising my need for comfort and counsel. It was nice to hear his reassurance that I would be free soon, and although my new journey may have bumps, it would end in a good, peaceful, happy place. I needed to hear that, and to this day I'm thankful for his kindness. A well-trained police force is invaluable for any person in peril.

Morning came. The girls got dressed and packed up their last few things, and we waited for my sister and an amazing family friend to come and move us back to our hometown. I spent time trying to make the girls giggle. I had to explain why we were leaving so much behind. They were concerned about what would happen to everything. I told them, "On our new adventure we don't need stuff… Just each other."

Right here, right now, get out the *Courage and Grace Workbook* and complete the exercise:

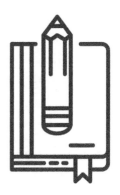

Your Breaking Point

When You found Your Courage

http://www.susanball.ca/your-breaking-point

Courage to Escape

> *"Above all be the heroine of your life, not the victim."*
> *Nora Ephron*

During my marriage, I contemplated escape, but my thoughts and society's expectations tricked me from the start. My mother had endured physical and emotional violence at the hands of her first husband and her second, my father. Years later she shared all the myths that kept her trapped. Her mother too, suffered at the hands of a vicious little man who believed it his right to keep his wife and kids beaten down and in their place.

When I met my abuser, I was vibrant, young, and single. I had left the father of my little girls because, while he was a good man, he lacked ambition, drank too much, and suffered from severe depression. We both agreed that was no example for small children to see. Never did I imagine I was exchanging my gentle but alcoholic first partner for the monster number two would turn out to be.

If you are anything like me, and the millions of women worldwide wounded by this epidemic, getting in was easy but getting out is difficult, and recovery, and reclaiming your joy will prove to be your greatest challenge.

Here's how it begins. Your abuse starts in drips and drabs. He makes fun of your cooking or the way you dress. He teases you for the words you say or retells embarrassing stories of your failures to friends. He's quick to ask you to move in, but he makes you work hard to be included with his friends, so much so, that once you're together, he suggests you stay home, relax, enjoy your time with the kids. After all, he's just joining the guys to watch the game, play a round of golf, or some such bull.

Somewhere in the back of your mind, you know better, but you comfort yourself with the fact that you're the woman in his home, his life, and his bed. And you begin to blind yourself to all that he is.

I was conveniently blind to his behaviour. After all, he loved my kids and me.

We all get into abusive relationships the same way: An abuser lies to us, makes us the kinds of promises we long to hear, manipulates our desire for the dream they offer and makes us pay at every step along the way. It's much like watching a gambler continue to bet on a bad hand, believing they have too much skin in the game to walk away. Let me tell you right now, this isn't a game, and if it were, it's one you can't win. Yes, you're all-in, but you'll lose. Once you draw the abusive relationship card, you're out, and you have lost everything you bet. Accept it. You need to, to move on.

I bet on a bad relationship, an abusive relationship, and I wasn't going to waste one more single cent of my life's potential on him. I was out, and so were my kids!

Right here, right now, get out the *Courage and Grace Workbook* and complete the exercise:

Your Escape Story

How I'm Celebrating My Courageousness

http://www.susanball.ca/your-escape-story/

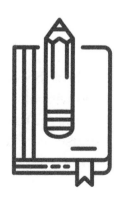

Darkness Into Light

There is a heaviness and a darkness that falls naturally upon us when we experience trauma of any kind. We retreat to protect ourselves. It's natural. When we're in an abusive relationship, we experience verbal, emotional, and sometimes physical attacks. The hurt and pain come from all directions and impacts every part of our physical and mental well-being.

After a while, we begin to believe that the easiest way to avoid these attacks is to toe the line. We see our environment like a combat zone, and the easiest and simplest way to keep the peace is to agree, apologise, and acquiesce. We do as we're told, when we're told, and how we're told.

During my darkest moments, I could not see colours other than black, grey, and red. Red for revenge. That colour popped when I thought of my abuser and my situation and how he was the reason why my life had become shit. Red was the only colour I saw.

The rest of the time I saw only black and grey. There was no colour in my thoughts, my imagination, and that made my future look very dreary, uncreative, and bland at best. Black and grey are the colours of hopelessness and depression. When you add a little dollop of red, it becomes the palette of the victim.

I walked through my days not able to see anything good or bright or hopeful in my future. I wanted to. I sat sometimes and tried with all my heart to imagine a happy future. The one I created for myself and my children. But the truth was my victim mindset was keeping me trapped in that black and grey world.

Me and my victim, we were simpatico, and it was easy to stay there. Comfortable. Relaxing. No work required.

No bothering with the deep internal self-healing work.

In the darkness, our voices become silent, and our dreams are lost. There comes a time when we don't even know who we are anymore. Our lives are committed to keeping the peace and accepting that the loss of our personal values, life, dreams, and voice is an acceptable casualty. But beneath all the layers of pain, hurt, silence, and sacrifice lives your true self. She's under there waiting to be released.

I want to guide you beyond the pain and hurt, toward a peaceful, joy-filled future.

I remember when I left my abuser, I fought to find JOY and HAPPINESS. Yet each was such an elusive target. Happiness? I wasn't even sure what that meant. And Joy seemed childlike and unattainable. I tried to be happy. Smiling at the right times. Being social. Dating. But it just felt empty. Without meaning or purpose. The feeling of happiness was fleeting.

I spent a great deal of time questioning whether or not I even wanted happiness. Was I ready to be happy? And through the process of writing and wondering, I discovered what I really wanted was PEACE. I wanted to make peace with my past, with my daughters, and most importantly, with myself. I wanted to wake up in the morning and feel peaceful, calm, and ready to embrace the day.

To find Peace I had to learn it doesn't stand alone. It is a combination and a balance of these 4 elements:

Curiosity: Are you curious about what you will create today? In your life? In your relationships? Curiosity plays a significant role in our mood and our overall enjoyment of the little things life has to offer.

As an example, I was invited to attend an opera. Instead of thinking it was going to be an endurance at best, I went with an open sense of curiosity, and I found myself really enjoying opera. When you open your heart and your mind to Curiosity, you'll be amazed at the adventures it will bring.

Authenticity: After an emotionally unhealthy relationship, we are left with a distorted view of ourselves. Usually negative, very negative and often extremely demoralising. Now is the time to reconnect with the real you. Your dreams, desires, hopes, needs, and wants. Take time to explore what you love to do. Say no to others so you can say yes to you. Love yourself unconditionally. Respect your opinions and your needs.

Gratitude: Be grateful every day for every small blessing in your life. Gratitude is healing, and it moves you forward to grow and prosper. There are no gifts in life without gratitude. If you've hesitated to board the gratitude train, I encourage you to hop on now. Learning to celebrate what you have is the fastest way to discover the life you want.

Happiness: Yes, it's an integral part of your larger peace plan. Liberally sprinkle your days with smiles, laughter, socialising, alone time, adventures, nature, food and all that makes you feel joyful is about building your happy life.

But What About Peace?

Peace is beyond happiness. It's that tiny square at the intersection of Curiosity, Authenticity, Gratitude, and Happiness. We find Peace when our life, happiness, and choices are not influenced by outside opinions and past reflections. When I discovered my desire for peace, I learned to let go, move forward, and thrive. True joy and happiness are not possible until you are completely at peace with yourself, your choices, and your past.

Time to release your victim story, and step into Fearless Confidence, Balance, and Wellbeing...

You did it. You took the first step and left him behind. I want to congratulate you for the courageous step in leaving that toxic, emotionally abusive partner.

It was a bad relationship, and you were consistently criticised, bullied, ridiculed, and abandoned. You decided it was time to say goodbye to your abuser and walk out the door. You decided you wanted and deserved a better life. And that's a good thing. But there is one small very dirty word that is keeping you stuck. Oh, it's a tiny little filthy word. It's a word that is short and pudgy. Only three letters that will keep you stuck in your rut forever.

W—H—Y—These three letters create one small depression enhancing word. A word that creates a never-ending loop. When you are stuck asking yourself WHY questions, you are stuck creating **Excuses**.

Fact—The only answer to a WHY question is an Excuse

When you are in an unhealthy relationship, it is very easy to get trapped in the Why Loop. You're looking for an answer, but it doesn't exist. You end up asking the question and answering with an excuse.

Why does he treat me that way? Because he's in a bad mood. Because his boss yelled at him. Because he had a long day. Because he hasn't eaten today. Because he's feeling sick. Because he's tired. Because he's a narcissist. Because it's too hot/cold/wet/dry outside. You can make up any excuse you want for him. In the end, each and every one is still just an excuse.

Why do I stay? Because I feel secure. Because I don't think anyone else will want me. Because I have no money or resources of my own. Because I'm worried about the children. Because, because, because.

Why does this always happen to me? Because I don't deserve good things. He says so. Because I brought it on myself. He says so. Because I'm stupid, and other useless and negative self-demeaning reasons that he gives me.

When we plant ourselves in the world of WHY, we do not come up with attainable goals to move us forward in life. We stay stuck hammering away at Why and trying to find the answer. It's a trick question. There is no answer, just excuses and debilitating negative self-talk.

Right here, right now, get out the *Courage and Grace Workbook* and complete the exercise:

Challenging the Why's

Identifying Your Curiosity, Gratitude, Authenticity, and Happiness

http://www.susanball.ca/challenging-whys

Kick Your Mind into Solution Mode

When you are in a bad relationship or suffer a setback, you can kick your mind into solution mode by changing the questions you've been asking yourself.

What – Where – How – When

When you leave a toxic, painful relationship, you leave with scars on your heart, but you also have **free will to create the life you love.** To fully embrace your new happiness, and heal the scars you have and to leave your story in the past. If you want the dream or even if you're just aiming for better, you have to let go of Why.

It's time to accept there is only one answer for what he did, and it is:

He is a mean-spirited dick who chose to demean and punish me without reason and whenever he could!

It takes courage and grace to let go of Why, but when you do, you'll enhance your life, capture your happiness, embrace and activate your big + bold + blissful story.

Right here, right now, get out the *Courage and Grace Workbook* and complete the exercise:

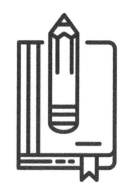

The Free Will Challenge

Identifying Your What, Where, How, and When

Creating your Big + Bold + Blissful Story

http://www.susanball.ca/free-will/

Courage and Grace

Chapter Two

MOVING WITH GRACE FROM BROKEN TO BLISSFUL

Let's talk about being stuck! I've been stuck, and it sucks. I was stuck at Broken. I was stuck at Victim. I was stuck at Depressed. You overthink, you bounce back and forth, and ultimately you can't make a decision.

Stuck is that place where you are when you are in-between, "I don't want to keep doing what I am doing, I can't keep doing what I'm doing, I don't want to go back to that..."

BUT, there's a really big BUT right here!

"I'm afraid of the future, I'm afraid to let go, I'm afraid of the unknown." And so you stay stuck in the same place and can't get out.

We know we're going in circles and that makes us feel our life is out of control. Feeling stuck is a symptom of the bigger problem at hand. It means that something has to change. It is a clear signal that you're resisting change.

It's scary to let go of something familiar and let yourself fall freely into your new story. But it is the best and only thing to do when you want to embrace and love yourself and your life unconditionally.

While you're holding on to your victim persona, you unintentionally close yourself off from all that's good. You have no room or ability for your Blissful Thriver to flourish. Consider your inner victim a shield guarding your heart and hope. That's great when you're in danger, but once you escape your abuser, you need access to what's behind that shield to heal and grow. You can't create unconditional self-love for yourself or anyone, including your kids, while your Victim Shield is firmly in place.

Releasing your victim is recognising your willingness to successfully take big, bold, courageous steps to freedom. When you do, you must celebrate your courage. You can create a life that has meaning and wake-up each morning ready for your next adventure. You'll know what you want, what is acceptable to you, and how you will achieve your goals. You will have taken back your power to create your life and freed your voice.

You will let your victim go. It's simply a question of when. How long do you want to be in pain before you choose? Yes, this is your choice, and it's for you to choose. I cannot express to you the joy and the fun you will have in your life when you decide to let your victim go. You will absolutely flourish. You will see how bright your future is and pursue it wholeheartedly.

I know it's scary. I held on for way too long, and when I look back now, I realise I wasted so much time and effort on anger, sorrow, and all the Whys of being a victim. Once you release your victim, you'll see all the possibilities that are available to you. Your heart will be open to grabbing on to them. You are amazing, and you're on your way to a fantastic life built by you and for you.

Being stuck is also where the greatest transformation in your life will happen.

When you feel stuck, it's a signal you need to get real with yourself, your situation, and how *you* are going to change it. Being honest is challenging. It can hurt. It can be painful. But once you sit down and get real, the answers come, and you begin to change your situation. And therein lies the road to Peace!

Wisdom Whisper

Be bold enough to use your voice

Brave enough to listen to your heart, and

Strong enough to live the life you've always wanted

Right here, right now, get out the *Courage and Grace Workbook* and complete the exercise:

Get Real Exercise

Write the Story Of You, The New You

http://www.susanball.ca/get-real

Getting Unstuck Starts Here

Step Away and Find a Place to Nurture Yourself

Change is as Good as a Rest, and when we step away into a new place—a coffee shop, a different room in the house, a park—your brain becomes stimulated by new sights, sounds and smells, and this inspires clearer uncluttered thinking.

Ask yourself honestly, what in your life needs to change?

Time to buckle up because this is where the rubber hits the road. What needs to change? What makes you feel unhappy? Or stressed? Or, has you shouting and raging? Or crying? Or uncomfortable in your own skin?

What's going on right now in your life that doesn't suit you and needs to change?

Write it down, honestly, and include all the dirty details. You really need to come clean and now is the time to do it.

Right here, right now, get out the *Courage and Grace Workbook* and complete the exercise:

My Life in Dirty Rotten Detail

Changes You Need or want

http://www.susanball.ca/dirty-detail

Who Are You Blaming?

Are you stuck in the blame game waiting for someone else to do something, anything, that will resolve your situation? Blame never works. You might not realise you're blaming someone else for your situation. If you are, this is your chance to recognise the truth and stop placing blame. Step away from blame and ask yourself "What am I going to do to fix this situation?"

Now you're taking personal responsibility, and that's where the magic starts to happen.

Switch it Up!

You probably do the same thing, in the same way, every day. Drive the same route to work. Tuesday is spaghetti night followed by hockey practice. Monday is yoga. Saturday is movie night. Let go of routine. Switch it up and add spontaneity and play to your day.

Take One Step

Make a commitment to taking a step toward change. One small step is all that you need to get started. With each step, you get more clarity about what needs to change and how YOU are going to change it to suit you.

Take an honest look at where you're stuck and then make a decision that will move you forward. It's your life. Set a goal and go for it. One step is all it takes to get you moving and away from stuck.

It's time to walk away from your victim'hood, love yourself unconditionally and embrace life fully.

Right here, right now, get out the *Courage and Grace Workbook* and complete the exercise:

Who Are You Blaming

Switch It Up

Simple Steps to Get Unstuck

http://www.susanball.ca/switch-up

The Broken to Blissful Method

How to Begin?

Moving from broken to blissful takes equal amounts of *Courage and Grace* to let "IT" go, forgive, activate your rebel self-love, and look forward to a big, bold, blissful future. Once you're committed to releasing your victim, you can embrace your blissful, thriving, courageous self. You are able to passionately create and enjoy every moment of life.

You can't change the past, but you can learn from it and change how you feel going forward.

Stepping into your Courage

This is that moment when you know you're better than all you've been told. You deserve kindness, love, peace, and happiness. This is the moment you decide to stand up for you and your children and say that's enough. This is the moment you actually walk out the fucking door and escape. This is the moment you take responsibility for your life and your happiness.

This is the moment you courageously take back your power and step into your fear on shaky legs and break free! Courage is giving you permission to Leave, Heal, and Create your life anew.

Have the courage to free your voice, be vulnerable, and leave your victim behind you.

Right here, right now, get out the *Courage and Grace Workbook* and complete the exercise:

Your Courageous Steps

http://www.susanball.ca/your-courageous-steps

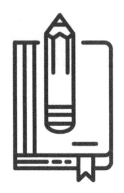

Free Your Voice

When I first started dating my abuser, there were a few events where my gut voice screamed, *"This is bullshit, run, Susan, run,"* but my conscious brain voice overruled with plausible excuses. I distinctly remember that he took me to meet his brother and his wife. I thought it was fantastic and a sign of commitment. Just a few days into our relationship and I was meeting his family. Sweet! But here's the kicker. When we walked into his brother's house, I remember the cone of silence. He and his wife literally stood with their mouths open like they had just seen a ghost.

My gut said, *"What the fuck?"*. No one was talking. His brother just stared at me. I felt so uncomfortable and disoriented. I had imagined sitting and having coffee and chatting with his family. Instead, it was awkward, silent, uncomfortable and a big warning. My gut said something was wrong but my mind made soothing sounds about catching his brother off-guard and they weren't prepared. So, I silenced my gut voice and didn't follow my instinct to question him about his family's reaction.

My abuser was married. Yup, married. In essence, he brought the "other woman" to meet his brother. Makes perfect sense why his brother and wife stood in shocked silence. I wasn't his one true love. I was the other woman to a married man with kids.

Listen. Listen very carefully because there is more than one voice inside us and each is challenging the other for supremacy.

OUR CONSCIOUS BRAIN VOICE

This is the voice filled with society's standards and expectations. It's your "should" voice, and the "what will others think of me" voice. It can be downright submissive.

    It's the voice of our moms, dads, grandmas, teachers, and other older adults who influenced our thinking as young children. They taught us rules and social skills and often times, it leaves us feeling unsure about taking a stand contrary to what we've been taught.

Right here, right now, get out the *Courage and Grace Workbook* and complete the exercise:

Who are You Listening to for Your Happiness?

http://www.susanball.ca/listening/

Our Gut Voice

This is the one that starts in your belly and feels like butterflies, and you want to let it out of your mouth, but your conscious brain voice suppresses it because it may cause upset or conflict.

Living in a toxic or abusive relationship, we constantly keep our gut voice to ourselves. We shut *her* up and shut *her* down. We keep that voice hidden, thinking it will cause another argument or degradation, or worse, a physical attack.

But that Voice, that Gut Voice of yours, is the most powerful weapon you have. When I look back on my abusive relationship, I think if only I had listened to my Gut Voice. What a different life I would have lived!

Right here, right now, get out the *Courage and Grace Workbook* and complete the exercise:

How to Out Your Gut Voice

http://www.susanball.ca/gut-voice/

GUT VERSUS EGO

The distinction between your Gut voice versus your Ego is fundamental to your peace and happiness as you create and write your new chapter. Ego and Intuition come from completely different places and are the exact opposite of one another.

Your Gut Voice or Intuition is based on love, joy, and finding true happiness in life from the inside out. When you are in touch with your intuition or your Gut, you rely on yourself and your decisions for your personal happiness and peace. No outside influence or opinions are needed. You know what you want, what makes you happy, and you work towards your goals. When you listen to your Gut, and you pave the way for your deep desires to be realised with conviction.

In opposition, your Ego, or conscious voice, is heavily influenced by the outer world. It's you seeking approval from outside yourself. This is where reliance on what other's think of you or say about you can destabilise your personal value. Listen carefully to yourself. When you're doing something to impress others or to gain positive attention, your ego is doing the talking. Some might call it "The Keeping Up With The Joneses' Mindset". Here's a little personal story demonstrating the conversation and the outcome perfectly.

My very first wedding was not to my abuser. I married a nice guy my family believed was good for me. I was pressured into marrying him because, according to my mom and aunties, I was 26 so what was I waiting for? He was nice, had a good job, what more did I want? Basically, they were telling me I would soon be too old, and my perfect dream relationship didn't exist. Just go for the basics, they advised – nice, hardworking, good natured, and...

I'll be honest and tell you I listened to their words and thought to myself, *What the hell am I waiting for? He has all the qualities of a "good husband."* So I decided that my family was right and it was time to get married.

I distinctly remember the glee from my mom and aunties. They were going to plan a big wedding with all the trimmings, and the whole extended family would be there, and we would all be happy and celebrate. **That was their dream.** I was the object at the centre of their plan. This would be the dream wedding they had all been denied. I felt like the stand-in bride, as valuable as the plastic bride on the wedding cake. Not once did I contemplate the marriage. This was all about the wedding.

I knew in my heart and my gut that I didn't want to get married and it became quite evident when shopping for my wedding dress. My entourage was my mom, my eldest sister, and four of my aunts – 4!!! We went to a popular bridal shop, and they were all so giddy and happy, and talking about how beautiful I would look, and all that Oh Happy Day shit!

The dresses were chosen for me, and I dutifully went and tried on dress number one. I can remember standing on a white pedestal in this beautiful gown will all these ladies staring at me and my mom's words, "Susan, you look bored. Brides aren't supposed to be bored. Smile!"

Even though my gut voice was screaming "Susan, stop this madness. Tell them you don't want to get married. You want to travel the world and explore. Tell them!" I said nothing. My ego or conscious voice would look around at all their happy faces, and I would think about the pain and hurt I would cause them if I cancelled the wedding.

I put their happiness and feelings before mine!

The big day came. As I walked down the aisle perched on my Dad's arm, face delicately covered by my veil, my gut voice was screaming, *Susan, you don't want to marry this man. Turn around. Run!* The tears started flowing and my Dad, bless his heart, knew exactly why I was crying. He put his big loving hands over mine and whispered, "I will walk out with you. I will stand with you. I will support you as you walk out."

My fathers' words spoke my truth. They were real and I wanted to turn around and run away but I looked at the groom and the people watching me, and I just couldn't do it. I was paralysed by indecision. The guilt and shame I imagined would come, drowned out my Gut voice.

Guilt, because I would hurt and embarrass a really nice guy. And he was and still is a very nice guy.

Shame, because I was silent for so long and let people plan this big wedding I didn't want.

Guilt, because my mom would be embarrassed in front of her family.

Shame, because I was weak and everyone would know.

As we approached the altar, my Dad slowed down and squeezed my hand and said, "Doll, it's not too late, but once I hand you over, there's no turning back." I told him I was okay but I wasn't, and he knew it. Without joy or hope for my future, I got married that day.

This was my first big lesson in listening to me, my gut, my intuition, and honouring that voice. No matter where you are or the test before you, you have choices. Make the choice that brings you joy first. You are not responsible for his happiness. You are not responsible for the happiness of family and friends. Listen to your gut and put yourself first.

Right here, right now, get out the *Courage and Grace Workbook* and complete the exercise:

Investigate the Times You Heard Your Gut But Listened to The Outside World and Your Ego/Conscious Voice Instead

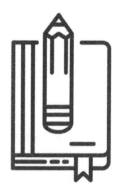

WHAT IS MY EXCITING, JUICY, HEART-CENTERED GOAL?

You must decide what you want, clearly and explicitly, and then fully commit to the outcome.

There is a huge difference between a wish and a commitment.

Answering your "What" requires honesty and sometimes painful introspection. You will be asking yourself, "How did I get here?" and "What events in my life had a significant impact. Are there relationships that I want to change? Or even eliminate? Is it time to move on, and move forward?"

Right here, right now, get out the *Courage and Grace Workbook* and complete these exercise:

What is My Exciting, *Juicy*, Heart-Centered Goal?

What Do I Want to Create in My Life?

Use lots of colourful details in your description. Remember, to be effective you must:

See it – Hear it – Feel it

ADOPTING GRACE

This is when you know in your heart it's time to heal the old wounds which led you into relationships that did not serve you. You understand that your old stories played a part in your past and now you gracefully accept your role as self-healer. You are working the steps of Grace into your daily life:

Grace to be You fully: You Say Yes and No with Equal Ease, Plan for Challenges and Embrace You and Your Victories. You are the Sole Creator of Your Big, Bold, Blissful Life. You are Authentic. Your Voice is Free, and You Use It.

GRACE has five equally important components:

GRATITUDE

I was presented with the idea of starting a gratitude journal when I was at my lowest point ever! I lived in a furnace room with two kids, no job, no money. I was hurt deeply by someone I thought loved me, but instead, he sent me running for my life. Lo and behold a friend said to me, "Start Practising Gratitude!" She really did in those exact words. My reaction was not pleasant, and a few nasty words were hurled in her direction. I thought to myself, *Are you fucking kidding me! I have nothing. What the hell do I have to be grateful for?*

Her next words were life changing:

> "You could start with being grateful that you don't live with him anymore and you are on your healing path."

Okay profound as her words were, I wanted to hate them. I really did. I wanted to ignore them and carry on in my *Victim'hood* and feeling sorry for myself. But try as hard as I could, I just kept thinking about her words, and she was right and...

I was grateful that I didn't live with him anymore!

My gratitude practice began right then, and it grew over time. At first, it was as challenging as my life situation, but every day I sat down and wrote five things that I was grateful for. As I carried on being grateful, my life started to change.

Gratitude Works and It Changes Everything!

I am grateful that at my lowest point, I was introduced to practising gratitude. It changed my life. It opened my mind and my heart to new possibilities. Gratitude and me...we go way back!

Creating True Happiness Begins with Gratitude

Take a moment now and open you *Courage and Grace Workbook* and complete the...

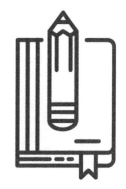

What Am I Grateful For...

Today, I am Grateful for...

Today, I am Grateful for...

RELEASE

I bet you're holding on to all kinds of negative junk. The junk you're holding on to is cluttering your mind and your path forward. Yeah, that's the truth! The things you hold on to, the grudges you bear or perhaps feel angry and hurt about, cloud your mind and prevent you from being the best you can be.

5-Signs You Are Guilty of Holding-On

1. *You won't stop talking about it, the incident I mean, your "IT". You want to tell everyone who will listen and even those who don't want to but are stuck! You get upset or angry when you feel you're not getting sympathy.*
2. *You fully embrace your victim label. You hold onto your story and keep telling it so you can rationalise your "victimness", you're hanging on for dear life.*
3. *You haven't moved forward. Not one little step. You can only be a validated victim if you stay right where you are. You have many excuses why you "can't" change or move forward or take responsibility for your happiness and life.*
4. *You haven't set any new goals. No new action steps to change your life. You haven't bothered to dream or rekindle a passion. Nothing. Nada'. You're just stuck.*

5. *You are losing friends, family, colleagues and acquaintances. People are jumping ship. No one has time for you and your victim story.*

When you leave a toxic, painful relationship, you leave with scars on your heart, but you also leave with your Free Will to Create a Life You Love. But to embrace your new happiness and heal your scars, you must leave your story in the past. You must let go of your victim; she's holding you back. It takes courage and grace to let her go. When you do, all the space she once occupied, is now available for your own use. You can create and enhance your life, capture your happiness, embrace and activate your big, bold, blissful story.

Holding on to what happened and being angry and bitter builds an unhealthy addiction to being a victim.

You don't need to know How to let go, you just need to be Willing.

Take a moment now and open you *Courage and Grace Workbook* and complete the…

**What Can I Let Go of?
Exercises**

AUTHENTICITY

The authentic self is the real, genuine you. It is the **You** that is buried deep and is at the very core of your being. The authentic self is a culmination of all things you are – your knowledge, talents, skills, attitude, and perspective. It isn't defined by your placement in a family unit or career. Finding the truth about who you really are and what is important to you takes honesty, awareness, and time. You are a lifetime journey. It's time to enjoy it.

 I allowed life's experiences, the opinion of others, and the abusive situations I survived, to bury my authenticity under piles of rubbish. Those were things I had been programmed to believe I couldn't do. There was so much negativity I attached to my self-image. There was fear and disbelief that I would never find me again.

But I did, and I'm amazing.

FIND YOUR AUTHENTIC SELF

So where do you find this authentic self? She's hiding under layers of protection and conditioning. To find **you,** you need to gradually strip away your layers of lies which you and the world have accepted. It's a process that begins with questions but not the ones you think.

"Today you are You, that is truer than true. There is no one alive who is Youer than You."

Dr. Suess

How do you know when you have successfully liberated your authentic self? Simple. It's when you can say 'no' without guilt, shame, or explanation. That's when you're authentic. It means you know what you want, who you are, and what makes you happy.

Right here, right now, get out the *Courage and Grace Workbook* and complete the exercise…

How Can I Be Authentically Me?

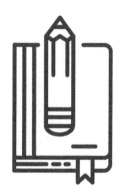

CHALLENGE

It is so easy to get stopped dead in your tracks when you start to think about all the challenges in your path. In fact, when you overthink your "to do" list, you could give up on your journey, and I don't want you to do that. Challenges are everywhere in life. Learning to face them is step one in overcoming any challenge.

It's not the challenge that keeps you stuck, it's how you handle it.

And the best way to handle challenges is to get out in front of them. Be clear about what you want to accomplish. Keep, delete, or edit your life like an interactive book. Then set goals to support your ideal outcomes. Big, bold, beautiful goals, worthy of your heart and hard work.

Challenges are easily overcome when they are changed into goals with an action plan. When we look at any challenge and ask "What can I do that will change this?" we immediately set a course of action. You can't change the outcome if you continue to do the same thing. If you want to face your challenges, do so with a plan, and set your course for success.

Challenges require Change and Change is Growth.

Take a moment now and open you *Courage and Grace Workbook* and complete the Challenge...

What Is My Next Challenge?

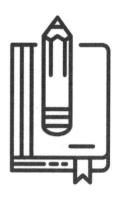

EMBRACE

While you were caught up in your unhealthy relationship, your life, your dreams and desires became your lowest priority. Now that you are free to Imagine the Possibilities. There are opportunities everywhere. You are free to choose which ones you will embrace and how you're going to invite opportunity into your life.

There is no one telling you what you can or cannot do. Breathe in the freedom and open your eyes, heart, and mind to all the fantastic choices that are waiting for you.

When you wake up in the morning, ask yourself: What Can I Learn Today? The answer is simply anything, everything or nothing. The choice is yours and yours alone.

It's Your Life Now.
You are FREE to do, be, and create a life that fills your heart with joy and happiness.

Take a moment now and open you *Courage and Grace Workbook* and complete...

What Can I Embrace as Possible? Exercises

Getting Your Life in Gear

I want you to rebel against your fears and know without a doubt that you can thrive after abuse. There are some who say that getting to the level of "Survivor" is good enough.

I say no way, not a chance!

Putting your life into Blissful Thriver gear is where you want it to be. After my experience with an abusive husband, I truly believed that my end-game was to go from victim to survivor and be happy with that. It was great to be a survivor, for awhile. But I felt uninspired. Something was missing, and I caught myself thinking, *Wow! I did all that work to get here, and now I'm a little bored.*

I discovered that I wanted more from life. I wanted to be more than a survivor; I wanted to thrive. I wanted a big, bold, ballsy life where I would flourish. If you've gotten yourself all the way to the level of a survivor, then challenge yourself to take your life all the way up to Blissful Thriver! I promise you'll be so happy you did.

Survivor versus Blissful Thrivers

Take a listen to your inner dialogue and make a note of your self-talk. Once done, read through the following statements. Notice the difference in the beliefs shared from each viewpoint. Is your inner voice speaking the words of a Thriver or still talking the limiting self-talk of a survivor?

Survivor: I don't deserve nice things. I'll never have a happy, fulfilling life. I know this is as good as it gets.

Blissful Thriver: Every time I wake up I feel Gratitude for everything in my life, big and small. I take the bad with the good because I know how to face a challenge and come out on top. I have the will to make each day a great success!

Survivor: She has low self-esteem and still has moments where she feels unworthy, guilty, or ashamed. She tells herself she "Can't". She's more afraid of what others will think or say and works hard to be unseen and unheard.

Blissful Thriver: She is vibrant and sees herself as an inspired, confident, woman. A fabulous woman! She knows that she is worthy of all the happiness, laughter, joy, and adventure now welcome in her everyday life. And she's willing and ready to go out and build her happiness.

Survivor: Her needs are right at the bottom. Saying no is almost impossible. She wants everyone to like her and avoids conflict at all costs. She tells herself things like "I can't…" using every excuse, but none are about her or her needs and desires. She's shut off from personal growth and frozen herself in time and place. As family and friends grow and change, survivors get left behind.

<u>Blissful Thriver:</u> **The thriving woman places herself first.** She knows that a happy, nourished self is the best one for her and her children. She's raising her kids to be strong and independent while she works every day to define her own path in life.

Blissful Thrivers are regular everyday women who have escaped the depths of hell. They have scars. They have pain, but more than that, they recognise growth and change are theirs for the taking. It's hard to stand up and take what you want, but Blissful Trivers want more and do. So should you.

You are Free Now. Free to Boldly Live a Blissful Thriving Life Created by You for You

Once you accept the role of Blissful Thriver your emotional, mental, and physical health will optimise. Daily irritations will turn into daily smiles and laughs. You will enjoy being with people. Equally, you will enjoy your company and be unafraid on your own. You will welcome being your own person again. You will confidently demonstrate to everyone how you are to be treated. Blissful Thrivers are in touch with their dream tomorrow. Being a survivor is only a stepping-stone on your healing journey. Choose to take one more step and push your life into Blissful Thriver gear. You are so worth it, and you deserve it!

It is so easy to "settle" for survivor. You don't have to face your fears. You don't have to step out of your comfort zone or step into your courage. You simply settle. As a Survivor, your victimisation becomes your story. The story you keep telling yourself is the story you keep living. Essentially, you accept the lie that you are not worth more. That you are not worth saying "yes" for and moving toward your big, bold, blissful goals and dreams.

But in settling, you also make an unconscious decision to "settle" across all areas of your life. Including intimate relationships. You give yourself an excuse to say "Oh, he'll do," or "This is what my life is like now."

And that's bullshit. Absolute bullshit!

There is One Question to Ask Yourself When You Believe Settling for Survivor is Good Enough

If this day were the last day of your life...

What would you want to be doing?

What would you want to be feeling?

Think about those two questions for a few minutes. Contemplate how you're feeling now in your place as a survivor. Consider how the label keeps you attached to your abuser. You live, walk, and breathe in the shadow of what happened to you. Is that okay with you?

Blissful Thrivers have stepped out of their survivor label by believing and accepting they are in charge of their happiness, goals, transitions, and life. They define who they are. They set the rules and boundaries for their life. They walk with dignity and happily step into their courage even though they are scared to death.

Blissful Thrivers are bold, courageous, and fearless.

EMBRACING YOUR BLISSFUL THRIVER

"Your greatest dreams are all on the other side of the wall of fear and caution."

Unknown

I believe that you are an empowered, confident woman who deserves a life bursting with positivity and happiness. It's time that you believe it too. I want you to experience that moment when you have butterflies in your stomach, and you're wondering what will everyone think. You start to question your motivations, and for a brief second, you think, this is crazy! Then it happens. You step into that fear with courage, you take a deep breath and say "Here I Go."

As you adopt Grace, and you take each harrowing step, you will blossom. You are stepping into your big, bold, blissful life. You are taking ownership of your happiness.

Keep going. You've got this!

Right here, right now, get out the *Courage and Grace Workbook* and complete...

Embracing Your Blissful Thriver

Yes or No, With Equal Grace

Sensational & Vivid Visualisation

Writing your *Exciting, Juicy, Heart-Centered Goal* is an important step in creating your life beyond the hurt, but it is only a part of the journey. To make your heart-centered goal an inseparable part of your everyday being, you need to bring it to life in all its sensational and vivid glory.

The Act of Visualisation

I love, love the act of visualising. We can close our eyes and create a vision of what we want in our future. We need to spend time visualising what we want to manifest into our life.

There is a fine art to the act of visualisation for the purpose of manifesting, and it requires using all five of your senses to get it right. No skimping. What you want to create needs to have feelings, colours, scents, tastes, movement and texture. It has to be the whole package, or you're going to miss out on a great big portion of what you really want.

I had a lovely client recently who was struggling with the whole process of visualising and had come to the conclusion that it was a crock. Some woo-woo crap that people were pretending to use but really weren't. We had a heartfelt discussion about the purpose of visualisation. She so desperately wanted to make progress and dug down to discover the details that had eluded her.

Her dream was a safe and secure home for her and her children.

She had recently left an abusive relationship and just wanted a home. In her visualisation, she would create a picture of a lovely house with a lawn and a front door that was just for her and her kids. She would focus on the house and use encouraging words about how she could and would make this happen. It was important to her, and it had to happen, but her vision was one-dimensional, just a desire for a house. There were no feelings or smells, or textures to give her dream depth, and in her vision, she never opened the door or crossed the threshold. She may as well have asked the Universe to keep her and her kids locked out forever!

I took her through a visualisation exercise that fired all of her senses until she could Hear, Feel, See, Smell and Taste the life her family would enjoy inside that house.

You can ask yourself these questions and create your own visualisation. The idea is to get your vision to pop! Make a movie of what you want to manifest and run that movie every day. Make sure you see **you** in the dream, participating, enjoying, inside the vision you want to manifest.

Questions to Create a Full-Blown 3-Dimensional Movie

1. *What colour is the house? See the different colours in the sunlight. Are there shadows from the trees?*
2. *Does it have shutters? Or a fancy mailbox? Add individual elements that reflect your taste and style.*
3. *When you walk in the front door, what do you feel? What do you see? Who comes to greet you? Can you hear music? Or laughter? Or peaceful quiet?*

4. *What do you smell? How does it make you feel?*
5. *Walk through the house to the living room and sit on the couch. Relax your shoulders. Breathe deeply and feel the texture of the fabric. Is it soft? Bumpy? Warm and comforting?*
6. *Stand up and walk through the house. Room by room. At each doorway, pause to enjoy each room. Notice the tiny things that make it your home. Touch and straighten up as you go along. Continue walking and moving through the house to the back door.*
7. *Walk outside and use all your senses to see, feel, hear, taste and smell all that nature has provided. The gentle breeze in the leaves. The smell of fresh-cut grass. The colours of blooming flowers. Relax and notice how calm and peaceful you feel.*
8. *This is your home, and it's filled with everything your heart desires. It's bright and colourful and filled with emotions, people, smells, textures and motion.*
9. *Now that's a sensational and vivid visualisation. There is a huge difference between visualising a house and seeing your life in your new home filled with laughter, music, food, and colour.*

The purpose of creating a vividly detailed visualisation is to get your juices flowing so you can see all the possibilities and opportunities that are waiting for you. Visualisation is about opening your mind to creating and being an active participant in the life you love. It is not about limiting yourself to a single outcome.

Visualisation is just as much about opening your heart to new possibilities as letting the Universe know you're ready for more.

Make sure that your visualisation includes you! Yes, you! This creates a positive association between you and the new life you are working to create. You are the central character in your movie. Make sure your opening shot features you. Add the kids, friends, and new possibilities but always start with you.

Oh, and while that white house with the green shutters you've been visualising may manifest as a pink house with lavender trim, that's okay. What's important is that you now have a house to live in and that signifies your life is improving and moving forward. You can always add green shutters at a later date. There are no rules other than to let yourself completely feel the vision you have created and trust that you don't need to know how.

The vivid pictures you create in your mind are movie-like and allow your brain to associate you living in a house, driving a car, laughing, and enjoying life. Anything you haven't done before can be visualised, opening the door to all your dreams and goals. Go all out. The colours and details you create, form an emotional bond between you and the goals you want to achieve.

Do not be fooled into thinking that if the house you are presented with is different from your visualisation, it needs to be rejected. It's the house that you want. The colour and detail in your mind-movie is simply the way to get your brain laser-focused on a home for you.

Right here, right now, get out the *Courage and Grace Workbook* and complete...

Creating My Fabulous Vision

TRIGGERS

Your Vision + Your Big Exciting Juicy Heart Centered Goal will keep you forward focused on your future, even when faced with difficult reminders or triggers. Your triggers are yours and yours only, and they bring up different emotions each time they fire. We have triggers attached to every human sense, and each can be activated by an outside source. A good example is, *Your Song* – the first few times you hear it, it will make you feel sad, and you will probably cry. The memories will be very heavy and emotional. Your heart will feel the sorrow.

Our song was Lady in Red by Chris DeBurgh, and I remember after I had run for my life it seemed to be playing everywhere and all the time. Of course, it wasn't, but with the heavy emotional attachment to the song and the tearful reaction it seemed to elicit, I just couldn't handle hearing it one more time without imagining my heart breaking.

Triggers are going to pop up while you're recovering and finding your joy and happiness. You may even feel like running back because your triggers are so powerful. I know when I heard that song, I longed for the dream I had been sold. Not the guy; just the dream. And that's what you're missing when you're triggered: You miss the dream.

The act of Sensational & Vivid Visualisation creates a new, vibrant dream that's all yours and you're in control of making it happen. Your happiness, your joy, your future is in your visualisation and glued onto your vision board.

Take advantage of these tools and give yourself all the help you need on your journey. As you work through healing and making your new dream life a reality, the pain of a trigger will diminish naturally. The dream he promised is no longer valid. It never was.

Your Big Juicy Heart-Centered Goal is Where You're Going + What You're Creating

Right here, right now, get out the Courage and Grace Workbook and complete the exercise:

Creating My Magnificent Soundtrack

How to Master the Fine Art of Trigger Swapping

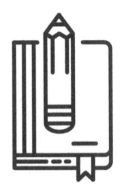

On Your Journey You Need to Celebrate

*It's Time to Smile and Say to Yourself
"Great Job, Keep Going, You're Doing Great!"*

Sitting alone in a furnace room, or running around in bars were indicators that I lacked connection. Real, sincere connection. I longed for human touch, compassion, and kindness.

When you are in an abusive relationship, you naturally disconnect from your abuser. You are abandoned in those moments when you need a hug or reassurance. There is no one you can count on to give you affection, a compassionate ear, or a warm hug with a tender smile. An abusive relationship is lonely. So fucking lonely! I thought he was my mate, my friend, my lover, and my companion but he was none of those things. As time goes by, the feeling of loneliness feeds your battered self-esteem causing you to shut down.

I can remember those moments when family or friends would visit, and I would sit there listening to their voices and their laughter. Taking it all in and trying to extend the time for as long as possible. Those moments were precious, and they made me feel human and worthwhile.

The hugs goodbye were long and sad. I knew in my heart that I would not be hugged until I saw them again. There was never a time I wanted to share what I was going through because I didn't want to bring negative energy to these fleeting, happy gatherings.

When you constantly have someone telling you that you're stupid, ugly, or a bitch, you start to believe what he's telling you is true. You soak in the negative crap about yourself, and you shut down further. You stop talking to friends. You stop engaging with the clerk in the store. You stop inviting family over for a visit.

You become disconnected from yourself and the outside world.

Healing from an abusive, toxic, or unhealthy relationship needs connection. It is essential to your well-being. As humans we crave connection and after a shitty relationship is when we need it the most.

Meeting new people takes courage, but there are a couple of ways to make your transition easier:

Volunteer

Charities, schools, local dance and art schools, even pet shelters desperately need volunteers to ensure their organizations run smoothly and efficiently. Things to consider before you make the plunge:

Does the organization engage in work that I'm comfortable with? If you don't like dogs, a shelter would not be a good fit.

Do they offer training and support for their volunteers? Look for opportunities to meet people who will encourage you to participate.

Will I be working alone? Some volunteer positions are solo gigs and will not help you overcome isolation and support your growth into unconditional confidence.

Will I feel pride in what I'm doing? Will you want to share what you are doing? Make sure you pick something that makes you smile, laugh, help others, and learn.

MeetUp Groups

These are great for getting out and meeting people. You can search local MeetUp groups in your city or town and do your research before you even venture out to participate. There are Meetup's for just about any interest or topic that you can think of, and there may even be one that supports getting over your nasty, unhealthy relationship.

The reason for volunteering or joining a MeetUp is that you will connect with new, positive, happy, inspiring people and situations. And that's what you need right now. New experiences with new people who are positive, happy and encouraging.

As you make new friends, join new groups, or take on volunteer opportunities, take a personal, heartfelt vow that your connections will be drama free. That means no talking about what happened. When someone asks how you are, you reply with, "I'm very well and thanks for asking." Every time you say the words "I'm very well," you reinforce your wellness and how good you are feeling. Give yourself permission to simply not talk about it.

If you are around people who constantly want you to discuss what happened in the past, disengage from them and spend your time with friends and family who encourage you and celebrate your life and you.

What you say and how you talk about your life has a direct effect on your outcomes and your happiness.

What you say re-affirms what is happening!

The funny thing about your mind is it constantly measures you from every angle. If you say, "I'm groovy today!" and paste a great big grin on your face, two things start to happen inside you. First, your mind reads your actions like sensor data: Smiling face, Increased heart rate, Vocal range in the happy zone; and it thinks you're happy and starts releasing hormones to support that activity. Yes, you will start to feel happy because you tricked your brain into accepting that you are happy. And, it gets easier. If you give your mind and body the basic permissions needed, you will start to feel happier and with that one little action comes the strength and grace to change your life.

Now if you insist on moping around, head down, thoughts turned inside and unwilling to enjoy even the smallest comfort or joy, your mind will interpret your wish and flood your system with emotionally crippling signals. Yes, you will literally be making yourself sick! You will find yourself exhausted and constantly in tears or worse, numb with pain and a loss of hope. As your depression worsens (yes, this is depression), your body will keep responding. You will feel lethargic and disinterested, even with things ultra important to you and your kids! If you keep this up, buckle your seat because a host of real illnesses will be in a hurry to make your acquaintance.

Think about it logically. Have you ever watched your kids at play? You know, when they're not showing off for you but really into their game, roughhousing, climbing monkey bars, or jumping from the dock into the lake? When you stand back and watch others, especially kids, having fun and completely enjoying the moment, it's hard to be depressed.

You must remember a time when you couldn't hold back a smile and a heartfelt laugh even on a bad day? Don't cut yourself off from enjoying life by closing off all your senses or denying your synapsis the very hormones needed to help you feel happy. Go ahead, say "I'm doing great. Thanks for asking," with a firm smile on your face and genuine gratitude in your heart and your mind will respond. After each greeting, you will begin to heal a little more, and in time, start to feel like your old self or even better.

And never forget to celebrate. You're taking huge, big, fantastic steps on your journey to wellness! You left your Tormentor. Celebrate that success every day! Celebrate every little step you take.

---

*It's hard to imagine your challenges as opportunities
but when you do, solutions will fall into your lap.
Sheryl Wright*

There will be challenges on your journey to Blissful Thriver. It's easy to be stopped dead in your tracks when you start to think about all the challenges in your path. In fact, when you overthink your To Do list, you could give up on your journey, and I don't want that for you!

Challenges are everywhere in life. It's not the challenge that keeps you stuck; it's how you handle it. And the best way to handle challenges is to get out in front of them.

No one reinforced that I was on a journey to an amazing life. No one said, "Hey, you can be anything you dream of and live a life that surpasses everything you had." No one said, "Hey, get out there, volunteer, meet new inspiring and positive people." No one showed me how to break down my challenges into bite size chunks so I could deal with them and get the results I wanted. I wish they had. My journey would have been shorter and my successes bigger. My celebrations more frequent and my gratitude journal filled to the brim. I could've had more time living a positive, happy, thriving life but you can if you're ready to learn from my mistakes.

This is the perfect place to stop and complete:

Your Future is Now Meditation Exercise

Click or Copy and Paste this link, to access the "Your Future Is Now" Meditation:

http://www.susanball.ca/yourfuturemeditation/

Right here, right now, get out the Courage and Grace Workbook and complete…

How to Know What You Want

My Immediate Goals

Celebrate Your Success

Courage and Grace

Courage and Grace

Chapter Three

How to Avoid Recapture

"There are no victims, only volunteers,"
J.J. Virgin

I escaped with my kids and a dream of starting over. We moved into my friend's furnace room. I was ever so grateful for that one tiny little space. I made life as normal as possible for the girls. School. Supper at the table. Activities. But what they didn't see was what happened after dark. Each night I left them to sleep in the care of my friend who was upstairs.

My nights were spent partying. Not just a few glasses of wine. I'm talking hardcore alcohol, drugs, and boys. I wanted the pain to stop and partying made it go away. But only for a moment. I was suppressing my anger and my hurt. I was masking it with alcohol I thought I was doing great and getting through it and doing the best I could and all the other lies we tell ourselves. But what I was doing was living the victim's dream life. I was free from taking personal responsibility. From looking deep within myself to heal the wounds of the past.

I would sneak home just before dawn and wash my face and try to look awake when the girls woke up. I thought I was winning. I was going to my court-ordered counselling and listening to all the other stories of horrible abuse and violence and sorrow. The best part of the counselling? I got to tell my story over and over again. I could cry and moan about how awful it was. And the others would nod their heads in understanding and sorrow. I didn't realise the counselling was a TRAP! The trap that leaves you wallowing in self-pity and the victim'hood.

What to Expect from Group Counselling?

During your one-hour group session, you are surrounded by your peers and led by a counsellor who specialised in domestic violence at University. Most counsellors have never experienced violence or betrayal or profound, deep gut wrenching hurt. My counsellor assured me she had read about it and wrote essays. So she was ipso-facto the expert. Bullshit! You need to believe in the people chosen to help you heal.

I stopped going to my group sessions and put my energy into partying. Why not? I had been given permission over and over again to continue living in my victim'hood. I could be a bitch to people and then tell them, "You have to understand; I'm a victim!" and with those magic words, I could avoid responsibility for my life, avoid getting a job, avoid moving forward.

More importantly, partying allowed me to avoid creating and designing my dream life. It kept me from experiencing true joy and happiness. Counselling had given me permission to settle for being a victim. Alcohol and bad boys liberated me from personal responsibility for the state of my life.

I had no reason to change.

I spent my days doing mundane tasks and plotting my ex's violent demise. It gave me great pleasure to create explicit downfall scenarios in all sorts of gruesome ways. It was going to be fabulous. He, my abuser, was going to pay for what he had done to my girls and me. All the energy I was spending on writing murder scenarios was keeping me locked in my victim story, and focused on the past and how I was going to get revenge. I was not focusing on the future or how I was going to get back on my feet.

On welfare, drinking, and partying too much, my cousin asked me to leave her furnace room because I was not getting a job. I got pissed at that and thought, *You rotten bitch! How kind of you to throw me out?* Again, I was wallowing in self-pity and blaming everyone but me for my crappy situation.

I moved to a basement apartment in a dumpy house. It was so damp Mushrooms grew on the bedroom wall. But I told myself it was all I could afford on my welfare cheque. Not once did I come out of my victim stupor and say, "Hey Susan! Wake up and get a job!" Nope. I was angry at what had happened to me, and I was going to enjoy being a victim. I was broke; living in a cheap dumpy apartment and the worst part was I didn't have anyone to look after the kids so I could go party. Just another reason to be pissed and blame others.

My desperate situation and lack of happiness and joy left me questioning my decision to leave. I felt like a fish out of water, flip-flopping, indecisive, and craving (yes, craving!) what I had left behind. The romanticised version kept me awake wondering and vulnerable to recapture.

In my victim state, it seemed so simple and easy to just go back to him. I would have financial security, and the kids would have a house with a backyard. Running back to that place would solve all my problems, and I wouldn't always be worried about money and feeling lonely and heartbroken. It seemed dreamy. Everything would miraculously vanish once I was back in the house with him.

But the desire to run back to solve your problems has one fatal flaw: you're relying on someone else to create your happiness, your financial stability, and your peace of mind. And that never works out in your favour.

"I've never seen any life transformation that didn't begin with the person in question finally getting tired of their own bullshit."
Elizabeth Gilbert

This is where my greatest lesson was about to be learned. The stark reality of self-responsibility for my happiness and security was about to rise up with a thunderous roar, courtesy of my youngest daughter, a little curly-haired blonde who asked me, "Can we eat the mushrooms growing on the wall? It would help us budget better!" That was a moment of clarity, and it pushed me to stop partying, face my situation head-on, take responsibility and look for a job. It was time to take full responsibility for my life, my happiness, and my future and my family.

The Three Myths

You escaped, now you're fighting for your happiness, stability, and life. In the beginning, it can be really hard to see any kind of viable happy future, and that's when you are most at risk of going back. After all, when you look back, you can see the home you created, a fridge full of food, the kids sleeping in their beds, their rooms full of stuff, and you dream about having stability again. You loved him once, and maybe if you go back, you can fix what was wrong and make it work?

"We either make ourselves miserable, or we make ourselves strong. The amount of work is the same."
Carlos Castaneda

There are Three Myths, three dangerous ideas, that make even the most courageous woman vulnerable to recapture. Your mental and emotional healing journey will begin when you honestly break down the three big excuses or myths that kept you locked in an abusive relationship or thinking of going back.

Myth One: I Love Him

This is one of the most pervasive of all lies we encounter and can keep us stuck in the cycle of abuse throughout our life. Love is one of the most overused words in our society. We're supposed to love our parents, family, and friends, but few prepare us to look out for predators within our ranks. We are taught to love our partner and many women still vow to obey a man. Our vows don't prepare us to defend ourselves from the same man if he should lie, cheat, or abuse us in his role as partner and husband.

Society is not on our side. Society is the woman who asks you what you did to deserve your abuse. Or the cop who tells you it's a waste of time to press charges. It's the doctor who buys your lies about your injuries because he's too busy to counsel you on your situation. It's every young man that thinks "Bitch" is an appropriate label for a woman. And it's every friend and family member who turns their back on you, telling you they don't want to get involved.

Love is not a campaign slogan or appropriate when applied to cookies, diapers, laundry soap, or any other consumer product. Yes, we can love our stuff, but in the end, the only true love is the uplifting, embracing, and enlightening emotion we arrive with at birth. As a baby and small child, we knew love, unconditional, perfect love. By the time we met our abuser, our understanding of love was twisted and manipulated to fit the lies of those around us who have already been bruised, battered, and sometimes destroyed by abuse delivered in the name of love.

Let's dive deep into the Love Myth first. It's the foundation of what we crave, but we may not recognise it anymore. We all believed we were in love with our abusers. After all, you would have avoided the whole situation if you knew in year heart what he was really all about.

In this section, I'll dive deep into love and identify all the imposters that have added to the lies we each believed.

Myth Two: I Stay for the Children

This is a painful, difficult topic but it needs a positive outcome. This lie has been around for so long it makes sense when we hear it. Who wouldn't put the kids first? Isn't this what you're doing? Statistics and generational abuse cycles all prove this is another lie.

Myth Three: I Have No Money, Friends, or Family

This myth is more about shame and fear and less about money or any other resource. It's also about the isolation he has created for you. Are you ashamed to call your family and tell them your idyllic life is a lie? Do you fear what your life will look like without all the trappings of your marriage? Are you scared your children will hate you for taking them away from their father or worse, choose to stay with him? You'll discover how this myth evaporates when you solve the first two.

I know each of the Three-Myths intimately. I thought I loved him. I so desperately wanted to make our family work. Ask yourself, is it **love** when you're **desperate** to achieve a goal or wistfully wishing for a positive outcome that's out of reach?

Abuse is not love, no matter what your abuser claims. Remember, you are not responsible for an abusers' actions. You did not make him this way, and you cannot change him.

My children had no say in who I married–I was an adult and could be with whomever I chose. Being an adult also meant I had to make the tough decision: stay and let them watch or leave and let them live in peace.

Money is the last of the great barriers, and I had none. Zero. But I had determination and courage. Was I afraid? You bet! The outcome I wanted for my life was in my hands, and I had to take control.

MYTH ONE

I Love Him

I remember saying to my sister, "But I love him!" Looking back at that moment, I cannot figure out what I meant. I know it sounds trite or strange or callous, but it's true.

What did I mean, when I was telling someone that I loved a man who strangled me and cheated on me?

Remember, by this time in my recovery from abuse, I had moved my kids into a dump telling myself it was all I could afford. A place so damp and dilapidated mushrooms were growing on the bedroom wall! And while I had escaped, all my attention and productivity were still being spent on him. I was still trapped but in a new kind of self-inflicted hell. One the courts, society, and even my friends imagined normal and acceptable for a victim in recovery from domestic abuse.

Today, years and miles from that place, I can still hear my youngest daughter ask, "Mommy, why don't we eat the mushrooms off the wall?"

Can you imagine letting your situation get so destitute that your child wants to eat mushrooms off the wall? I mean what was I thinking! Not much. Just the ever present song and story I had been taught by the courts, the police, and my group counsellor: **"Susan Ball, you are a victim of domestic violence."**

And then the worst thing happened—he, my abuser—called me and said he was in Toronto and would love to see me. He missed me. He loved me. He made mistakes. And I fell for it.

I actually fell for it!

I lied to my mom to get her to babysit, and I went out and met him. I remember getting all dressed up and I thought, I feel alive. I'm going to get him back, and this nightmare will be over. I get to go back to my house and be a mom and wife. It will be lovely…

I couldn't be more wrong!

We met, and it was all lovey-dovey for a brief minute. We chatted and ate dinner and drank wine. And at the end of the meal, he said "Did you happen to pack the video camera when you left? I've been looking for it."

I don't think I can describe how I felt at that moment but I knew he had not come to get me back. He had blatantly lied so he could get the stupid fucking video camera! I got mad, and for the first time, I let him have it. My feelings, my anger, and my hatred came out in a steady violent stream of words. At the end of my tirade, he asked, "Are you done? Good. You don't have the camera, and I don't have time to drive you home."

That was it. I was left standing on the sidewalk outside a restaurant late at night and had to find my way home. I cried and cried and cried for days. I wrote the most vicious, gory, blood-curdling revenge scenarios. As the days passed, I wept less often, and my need for revenge started to abate. I knew this time was different; I was beginning to heal. I still drank a bottle of red wine every night, but something was changing.

What is Love?

One of the most common phrases I hear from women who are staying with their abuser is, "I Love Him." Well, that may sound all Cinderella and lovely, but it's a very misleading and dangerous statement. You see, the idea of love is incredibly powerful. When we believe we love someone, we will stop at nothing to make sure they're happy, healthy, content, and peaceful. We will serve their every need selflessly. And being the nurturer's we are, we often put our personal well-being and needs on the side burner while we tend to our loved ones.

In an abusive, manipulative relationship Love is not what's happening. Not at all.

Your abuser has taken the time to make you rely on him for everything. You are dependent and needy. He has shattered your self-worth, self-esteem, and any other part of you that he wanted to break. That's how they get complete control of you. It's not love you feel for your abuser, it's **dependence**. Pure and simple. He has worked very hard to make you dependent.

Your heart races when you think about leaving because you're scared. What lies on the other side? How will you support yourself? Where will you live? What will others think about you? Questions, questions, and more questions, and none of them seem to have an answer. So it's easier to stay and say, "But I love him." Deep down you know that's not true, but it's easy. It's simple. It solves your immediate needs. You feel comforted. You feel you can put up with his violent, destructive outbursts because you love him. You tell yourself, the outbursts are the **worse**, in the **for better or worse** part of your vows. And true love heals and mends so you stay to fix him, to heal him.

Completely disregarding your needs and ignoring how lonely and unloved you honestly feel.

I vividly remember believing with all my heart that I was in love with my abuser. I actually thought that if I stayed and nurtured his good side, we would survive and our marriage and love would prevail. The truth is that no matter how hard I worked to convince him he loved me and wanted me, it would never happen, simply because I didn't love myself.

Among our greatest challenges in life are self-examination or being honest with ourselves. Taking responsibility for our happiness is the biggest and most daunting. Your partner, your friends, your parents, or your job, are not responsible for your happiness. Only you are.

It's time to get out the *Courage and Grace Workbook* and complete the…

**What the Hell
Do I Love About Him?
Exercise**

Why Making Him Happy Doesn't Bring Happiness

I wanted so badly to be "in-love," to feel love, that I mistook all the warnings of abuse for signs of love. I gave up my dreams, my aspirations, my goals, and anything that brought me joy in an attempt to make him so happy he would love me unconditionally. I vividly remember sitting at home thinking it would be so nice to take an art class. Watercolour painting to be precise. The town we lived in had a lovely art school, and they offered inexpensive classes. I love dabbling in art and creativity.

One day, while the girls were in school, I walked over to the art studio to talk about classes, the costs, when, and if you had to have experience. It was so exciting to be in the school. All the possibilities were right there in front of me just waiting for me to pick one. I chose watercolour painting and gathered all the information brochures to take home. I was singing and humming and laughing with the kids telling them how I was going to paint beautiful pictures and be a millionaire and famous.

He came home after work, and while the girls were at the supper table, I burst out with great joy telling him how I had discovered art classes, and they were reasonably priced, and how excited I was. His reaction was less than supportive. It was downright cruel. He laughed and said I was an idiot to even think he would pay for me to fail at art or anything else. I was deflated. I did not stand up for myself. Instead, I thought, well he does so much for us, and he's probably right that painting class would just be a waste of money. I wanted him to love me, so I did it his way. That was a mistake. Every time I let go of my dreams, desires, and joy and did it the way he wanted it done, I lost a piece of myself. And in some cases, it was chunks. Great big beautiful chunks.

He didn't love me, period. And not going to art class was not going to change that. You give up, give in, bend over backwards, and forget about yourself as you cook, clean, and look after the children. And all to get his attention and his affection. You're giving up on yourself, hoping he will notice you, be kind to you, and most importantly, love you. Still, love doesn't come. Oh, there are a few fake moments, but he uses those to get his way.

Life is way too short to be with someone who disrespects you and treats you like an afterthought, or a punching bag, or someone to verbally assault and belittle. Someone who abuses you doesn't like you. You have the ability to quit your addiction to your abuser and move on and find real happiness.

Motivational Tip: Always remember, you didn't break your marriage vows to your abuser by leaving. He broke his vows the moment he started abusing you, or cheating on you, or disrespecting you.

Rebel Self-Love

"Fear holds us captive, but self-love sets us free."
Susan Ball

Healing is all about how you **honour & love yourself**. It's time to rebel and love yourself unconditionally. Deep self-love shows others how you expect to be treated.

It's impossible to find a truly loving, equal, and respectful relationship if you're not in love with yourself. When you love yourself, you say yes and no with equal grace and ease. Self-love is uplifting and comfortable. You'll know who you are and what you'll accept. Your life will become balanced, loving, and happy. It's time to invest your love in yourself, to fall madly and truly in love with you.

Rebel Self-Love is an equal mixture of confidence and worth.

Confidence – memory of success. Every time you successfully complete a task, you build your confidence knowing you are now capable of that using that skill.

Worth – the value you put on yourself. How you cherish yourself, your life, your thoughts, your body, everything little bit of you. How you embrace your unique quirks.

Worth and confidence are synchronised and are uniquely different at the same time. They work together to create boundaries, and they're what you deflect the outside world. When you value yourself, your beliefs, and your desires, setting boundaries and sticking to them is a piece of cake. There is no second guessing your decisions when you know what you want.

Building your self-worth, how you value and cherish yourself starts with flirting. Bizarre, I know. But that's where it begins. Look in the mirror and give yourself a little wink or smile and say out loud: "I Am Worthy. I Am Valuable." Finish with a little air kiss. Straighten your shoulders and walk tall. You Have Value. You have worth. Let the world see it too.

Right here, right now, get out the *Courage and Grace Workbook* and complete the exercise...

I Am Worthy

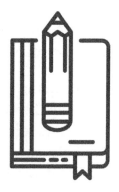

Rebel Self-love is not selfish. It doesn't mean you should adopt a bitchy attitude. It doesn't say that you think you're above anyone else. It just means that you are a priority in your life. You give yourself the attention you deserve.

I want you to tell yourself, "I choose me." This is not selfish. Repeat: "I choose me, and this is not selfish. I choose me, a happy, healthy me!"

Choosing yourself is the only way to heal, grow, and Thrive!

What You Reflect, You Attract

It's a truth you can't skip. Part of the reason you found yourself in an abusive relationship, was your willingness to put others first. Don't blame yourself. We women have been conditioned since birth to put ourselves second. We were told by our mothers, our family, our community, and society that we come second. It's a promise they made, that as long as we put ourselves second a man will step up and care for us. It's a pervasive message. So pervasive, we see it everywhere, movies, TV, advertising, you name it. How many of you have been told "you can't," simply because you were born a girl?

Being born a girl stopped me from pursuing my dream vocation. I wanted to be a veterinarian from the time I was old enough to talk. My dad took me to see movies about wild animals, and we watched documentaries together about domestic creatures in need. I wanted to be a vet. Period. And that was my one and only career goal.

I focused my studies on the sciences and passed with fantastic grades. I wanted to make sure that I was accepted into Veterinarian College without any issues or setbacks. I studied, and I learned, and I read, and I moved closer to the goal.

Until the fateful day at the age of 15, I met with the Guidance Counsellor at my school. My dad was with me because it was the day we would all discuss what I wanted to be and how I would get there. It was important that a parent be there to hear all the nitty gritty details and requirements. I blurted out "I want to be a vet!" fully expecting that the counsellor would be pleased I knew exactly what I wanted, and he could show me the way.

What actually happened that day was a young girl, and her dreams were crushed. I was told that "girls" were not accepted into veterinarian school. Only boys! I vaguely remember them talking about Secretary or hairdressing school or perhaps I could be a nurse. Sexist? Just a little. I left that day with an armful of brochures and a broken heart.

This was a body blow to my self-worth and my confidence and my esteem. My dream, my hard work, my future was taken from me, and I had no say.

I was made to feel less valuable just because I was a girl.

It is events like this ladies, that wear away at our self-worth. We start to like ourselves less, and we start to question our value to others and how it's measured.

Growing up is a litany of You Can't, You're Not Capable, You're Not Wanted, You're Not Allowed, and all of those statements lead to one huge overwhelming limiting belief:

I am less valuable

When we have low self-worth and don't cherish ourselves, we look to others to fill the void. To boost our worth. To cherish us. To love us. And predators – those mean-spirited, abusive dicks – can feel our vulnerability, and that's how we get hooked.

Healing begins by recognising, naming, and accepting our limiting beliefs. I prefer to call these limiting beliefs the stories we bought into which diminish our sparkle. Once we know our false stories, we can set the record straight by replacing them with empowering and authentic stories that liberate our rebel self-love and inspire us to take action to pursue our big, bold, blissful lives.

Oh, and there is no age limit on big, bold, and blissful living. It's never too late to start back on the road to your old childhood dreams. John Glenn was 72 when he flew on the space shuttle and Canadian Roberta Bondar, is in her seventies too and still active in the space program and training for another year-long mission to the space station.

Nurture your self-love, and you'll develop unstoppable self-worth that will keep you free from toxic or abusive relationships and put you back on the path to actively embracing life and all it has to offer.

Right here, right now, get out the *Courage and Grace Workbook* and complete the exercise...

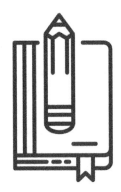

Rebel Self-love Exercises

LAUNCH YOUR GREATEST LOVE AFFAIR

"Perhaps we should love ourselves so fiercely, that when others see us, they know exactly how it should be done."
                                        Rudy Francisco

One of the greatest lessons I learned from my incident was that I did not value myself. Hell, I didn't even like myself. I didn't respect myself, and my sense of self-worth was garbage.

I had no idea!

I thought I was confident and capable and worthy, but the terrifying truth was exactly the opposite. Getting to a place where I love myself unconditionally meant I had to dive deep into my limiting beliefs—stories firmly entrenched in my being. I had once absorbed those stories and lived a lie based on the deficiencies I was told I had.

True, meaningful self-love is only alive within you when you recognise and heal your wounded inner child. What does that mean? It is a process of remembering and recognising life changing moments and events from your childhood. It is not about blaming anyone for what they did. It is only in recognising, acknowledging, and accepting that what went down affected you deeply and remains in your subconscious directing traffic.

Your wounded inner child could be the result of negative attention, demeaning comments, incidents of bullying, physical or sexual violence in the home, abandonment, continuously moving and changing schools, or being teased and ridiculed because you are different in some way.

I know firsthand how painful it is, but I'll give you a shining example from my childhood that attracted the monster but first, an exercise:

Right here, right now, get out the *Courage and Grace Workbook* and complete the exercise:

Recognizing & Healing My Child Wound

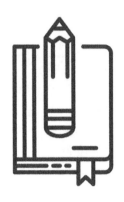

Unwanted and Abandoned

I was child number five during a time when women didn't have access to birth control. My parents were in an ugly relationship, and I was a huge inconvenience. Arriving in their mid-thirties, my parents were not interested in raising another child. My closest sister was ten years older than me, and my eldest sister was fifteen years my senior. She was old enough to be my mother!

So, along comes a baby into this fiery, rocky marriage. My mom wanted her freedom, and a new baby gave her exactly the opposite. By the time I was eight years old, my parents were divorced, my sisters had married and moved out, and I was shipped to the neighbours' house to live. The neighbours!

How unwanted and abandoned can a child feel?

I did not recognise that this event in my childhood solidified my feeling of unworthiness. As I child I had no way of understanding this wasn't about me. In my little mind, I must have been really bad or ugly or stupid for my parents to send me away.

That childhood perception of myself was buried deep in my subconscious mind, the place where our brain works to manifest our beliefs.

Thirty years pass and I have two girls of my own and along comes a man who offers a home, forever love, companionship, and security. I was the perfect victim for him. I was so desperate to feel wanted, loved, and needed that I could easily overlook his lies and manipulations. Abusers are masters at cracking your self-worth issues and using them against you. There is a direct connection between self-love and standing up for yourself. I was too broken to stand up to his bullshit. When he called me ugly, I just collapsed because it fed my deepest worries and confirmed my abandonment story.

If I had the Rebel Self-love I have now, I would have instantly told him that insulting me was unacceptable on any level, and at any time, period! I would have set the tone of mutual respect and consideration at the very beginning of the relationship. I would have had an active, strong personal voice, and I would have used it without hesitation.

The truth is, the woman I am now would never take a second look at a man like that today. Oh, my ego might have enjoyed the attention of a handsome, rugged man on a night out dancing with my friend, but it would have ended there. A few kind words from a stranger are nice to hear, but I would have recognised the play, the moves, even the compliments for what they were. I would have known how to say, "Thanks, but no thanks," and I would have had the courage I needed to turn and walk away.

It will hurt to open your childhood wounds, closely examine them, and ultimately, heal them. Addressing the limitations drilled into us since birth can become a lifelong occupation and lead us back to the blame game. You don't need to go there. Your mom, dad, grandparents, teachers, religion, media, and community all imposed their beliefs on you. They didn't mean to and in most cases, were just passing on all the limiting beliefs that had once been dumped on them.

Your job is to simply listen, acknowledge, and allow your inner child to heal.

Begin by accepting your limiting beliefs were instilled in you just as they were your parents, friends, and community. Over time, those limiting beliefs settle into your subconscious mind, where they become your common truth.

As children, especially small kids, we have no filtering system to judge the beliefs passed on to us by those we trust. If someone in authority, a parent, teacher, cop, tell us we're stupid, we will internalise it. If the negative belief is repeated, our little self is programmed to accept the situation as true.

If you insist on playing the blame game, try figuring out where your parents, their parents, or their parents accepted the limiting belief you're now trying to overcome. You could find yourself going back generation after generation. It's up to you to stop the blame game and start creating new empowering beliefs that serve you and in time your kids.

When you acknowledge and accept the situation as being out of your hands just as much as it was with your mother and her mother, and so on, you begin to do more than heal, you start to grow. You are creating a new reality for you and your kids, a new unlimited world. When you replace those old limiting beliefs, you allow your inner child to heal and grow from that place, and you begin to shine in your true, vibrant self.

We attract what we reflect. If we're reflecting loneliness, unworthiness, and neediness, you will continue to attract predators and have unsatisfying, hurtful relationships. Your relationship with yourself is the most important one you will ever establish. It reflects who you are and how you expect the world to see and treat you. And it's what attracts others to you.

Self-Love is Confidence

After all, you spend 100% of your time with you. Wouldn't you rather spend time with someone who is supportive and appreciates just how awesome you are, warts and all? Of course, you would.

Rebel Self-Love is you falling deeply, madly, in love with your amazing, audacious, gorgeous, unique and beautiful self.

The Major Benefits of Unconditional Self-Love

1. *You get to set the example for how you are to be treated. No exceptions*
2. *You have secure boundaries, and you confidently assert yourself*
3. *You can say yes and no with equal grace and ease*
4. *You attract like-minded individuals into your life as equal companions, sharing life's journeys*
5. *You are your fiercest cheerleader! You don't look outside yourself for validation or happiness, you create it from the inside!*

Rebel Self-Love Exercises

Right here, right now, get out the Courage and Grace Workbook and complete the exercise...

How Would Rebel Self-Love Make Me Feel?

What's holding you back from practising self-love?

NURTURE YOUR SELF-LOVE

Taking time for self-love is a healthy way of nurturing your connection with self and deepening your personal commitment to your values and happiness. Your relationships—personal, financial, business—are a direct reflection of how committed you are to *you* and what *you* stand for. To deeply nurture and understand your values, you need to take time for self-reflection and connect with your thoughts, emotions, and dreams.

To get you started, here is my personal list of activities I consider deeply nurturing and healing.

4-Self-Love Activities to Nurture Your Connection

Nature—any time I spend outdoors boosts my spirits, relaxes my mind, and inspires me to just be. Nature is my encouragement to live in the moment. To go with the flow of my emotions and listen to my heart. Nature is a healing force that I seek out regularly.

You needn't go far to put a little nature in your life even if you live in a big city. Find a park bench near a big old tree and spend some time just breathing. Perhaps your town has a Butterfly Garden, Conservatorium or Arboretum? Even a visit to the local big box garden centre can be uplifting. If it's your only connection to nature's world, grab a cart and spend some time looking at all the plants and shrubs. You might even take your time to note your favourites in your journal or snap a few pictures on your phone to add to your vision board for when you get to landscape your new home.

There are always little ways to find what you need if you try.

Technology Disconnect—I schedule time in my day, every day, to disconnect from all technology—TV, internet, games, phone—all of it shut down, turned off. While they're turned off, I can turn on my instincts, my soulful self, my dreams, and my desires. I can quietly and peacefully connect with me on a deep and personal level.

One important note on staying connected these days. When we're connected, we're at the world's beck and call. We all do it every day. When we connect, we work at the discretion of the world around us. Whether it's work, the kids, your mom, the women from your support group, email, papers that need to be completed, it goes on and on, and when we answer these demands first, we are putting ourselves on hold. That doesn't mean you don't connect or get anything done but you must consider your needs too.

When you disconnect, you create a moment in time where you are available for you only. Be self-seeking. Set aside a few hours every day, preferably before you connect. Use your time to read and write in your journal, create a new vision board, meditate, or workout. This is not selfish. You need to make you better, stronger, and healthier, not just for you but your kids and your future. Setting aside time for just you, each day tells your mind and your heart you matter. It gives you the time to define what you want and allows your new dream to coalesce in your mind and your heart.

A Date with Me—each week I mark time to go out with me. Some weeks it's only thirty minutes. Other weeks I designate the whole day. On my dates, I take myself out for lunch, to the movies, to an art gallery, or to a park. I respect myself and my time by never breaking or postponing my date. I wouldn't hurt myself like that. I'm teaching myself, I can be that friend we all want to have lunch with or join for a movie. Self-reliance, self-respect and nurturing self-love are all outcomes of a date with me.

You may assume this is the same as my suggested time for you before you reconnect with the world but it's entirely different. You can easily spend your daily disconnect time at home, but a date with yourself should involve leaving the house. You can't hide. You may want to spend your days wallowing at home with your head in the sand. It's a normal stage but to heal you must get out and you need to do it on your own. TV, Social Media, and the kids are no match for the real world. A date with yourself is about getting out of your laundry clothes, doing something with your hair, and walking out the door knowing you made an effort for you and you alone. Consider this your weekly exercise in proving you're worth your time and effort. Have fun, explore, and discover just how much you like yourself.

Gratitude—my daily practice of gratitude helps ground me in all that I am. There is always something to be grateful for. I have had dark times in my life and was able to reconnect with my happy, joyful, loving self through gratitude. Do it. It works.

Practising Gratitude can be as simple as telling three people something you are thankful for every day. Many people keep a gratitude journal where they write three entries every morning and every night. This is a great practice that sets your mind into a mode of thankfulness before you fall asleep. It helps clear all the extraneous negative things racing around in your head. Many women who keep a gratitude journal and apply the practice every night tell me they sleep better and wake up in a positive state, ready to face the day.

Your Gratitude Journal need not be a work of art, but there's no rule that says you can't have fun with it. You can pick up something cheap at the dollar store or grab something fancy from the bookstore. Hey, you can probably get all sorts of scrap paper from the local printer and staple something together or put those pages in an old binder. Whatever you choose to do, make it yours and remember, this is a simple exercise in propelling your fabulous manifesting mind into positive territory. It's where your mind needs to be if you want to open up to new opportunities.

These are my four activities to nurture self-love and honour your commitment to becoming your own best friend and advocate. Use them, and modify them to make them your own, or create your own from scratch. The important message is that we all need to be our own fierce, devoted cheerleaders. Your date with yourself is a commitment to you. Keep it! If you cancel or change or simply ignore your commitment to self-care, you're dishonouring and disrespecting yourself

I remember my first date with myself. I felt so uncomfortable, selfish, and foolish. I sat on a bench and interrupted my negative self-talk with kind words. I think my lips sometimes moved alarming people walking by, but it was all for the greater good. My greater good. I pledged my commitment to me, creating my new life, and my self-worth.

Make a deep, loving commitment to cherish and honour yourself every single day.

MYTH TWO

I Stay for the Children

Are Your Children at Risk?

There is so much confusion, and commentary, around this issue. Staying or Leaving? Which is better? And how do I know what is right for me? I want to create a nice little scenario that will offer clarity on the issue of staying for the children.

Consider This: Your kids hear you arguing, and they can feel the tension between mom and dad. They are exposed to your anxiety when you hear his car pull into the driveway or during dinner. They have no words to articulate how the violence, name-calling, bullying, and tension is impacting them. No words. The emotions are too complex for children to understand or express. They have not yet learned how to comprehend complex adult situations. They must convert what they are witnessing, using their only tool, a simplified child-view of cause and effect. And when they do, they do so by applying fault to themselves, their siblings, your abuser, and sometimes even you.

> *"Children of abuse feel isolated and vulnerable. They are starved for attention, affection, and approval. Because mom is struggling to survive, she is often not emotionally present for her children. Because dad is so consumed with controlling everyone, he also is not present for his children. They become physically, emotionally, and psychologically abandoned."*
>
> *(Roundtable)*

Here's what they do know: Mom is hurting and crying. They have no way to help you or comfort you or fix the situation. They are experiencing a new type of helplessness. And they are torn between their parents. They don't like their dad when he's hitting mom, but they're too little to get him to stop and they sure as hell don't understand. Did they do something to cause it? Did a sibling? For children, Cause and Effect are literal things and apply to them first, in their own little world.

I lived in abuse, believing my kids were less exposed if I sent them to their room, or a friend's house, or asked them to go outside and play. I thought if they couldn't hear the nasty, ugly names I was being called, or couldn't see the physical attacks, our fighting would have no impact on them. I thought they would be okay if I could just keep everything out of sight. I was sure I could keep the abuse in my marriage a secret from them.

It was a lie. A nice fat juicy lie I told myself every day!

In fact, I can see clearly how the tension, violence, and continuous emotional upset in the house affected my kids. The youngest pee'd the bed every night. The anxiety and fear she felt caused her to hide her wet pyjamas and underpants. She was terrified to tell anyone for fear of causing a fight that would hurt her mom. My eldest daughter did everything in her power to protect her baby sister. She would take her upstairs to watch a movie or just to play. She would hug her and tell her "I Love You". She was taking on the parent and protector role for her sister.

The kids knew everything!

Your children see, hear, and feel everything. There is nothing you can hide from them. They are intuitive little humans, and they can see the pain in your eyes. You are not fooling them. But you are teaching them that it is acceptable to exert control or relieve stress by using violence, or that violence is in some way linked to expressions of intimacy and affection.

> *It's estimated that more than 275 million children worldwide are currently being exposed to violence in the home. UNICEF calls this epidemic, "One of the most pervasive human rights violations of our time."*
>
> Brian F. Martin,
>
> *Founder of Children of Domestic Violence, a New York-based nonprofit organisation*

You may believe that you are providing a home and a family for your children but what you're giving them is a legacy of drama, chaos, and violence. And that's not healthy for them or you.

Getting a divorce is not what you planned. You married for life, but you have been deceived by your partner and your children are now the innocents who are witnessing their dad or step-dad calling you names, putting you down, ridiculing your abilities, and hitting you. That is not cool, and you are not to blame, but you can change your child's living environment and teach them that abuse in any form or manner is wrong and unacceptable.

Remember, your children did not choose this life. Is a legacy of abuse what you want them to receive?

Let's Go to the Movies Scenario

You're sitting at home watching a movie with your children. In the movie, a scene starts to play out where a woman is being belittled and slapped around. You realise there is going to be more violence, and the language is foul. Do you:

A. *Let them watch. What the hell. They might as well learn now how bad it can get! Or,*

B. *Turn the movie off because you don't want your children watching a woman being assaulted? Or,*

C. *Explain to your children there is no excuse for anyone to speak cruelly to anyone and hitting is definitely out of the question?*

Most people will answer B or C. I haven't had anyone tell me A was acceptable but if you are allowing your children to live in a home where you are verbal, mentally, and physically assaulted, that's the message you're giving them.

How else would you explain it? It's not okay in the movies, but it is at home?

Stop, close your eyes, take a deep breath, and ask yourself how you justify keeping your children in an unhealthy relationship? Be naked, raw, and honest when you answer this question. Otherwise, you're continuing the lie you've been telling yourself about the well-being of your children.

What Have Your Children Already Witnessed?

- ☑ *Bullying?*
- ☑ *Physical Violence?*
- ☑ *Bruises?*
- ☑ *Tears?*
- ☑ *Fear?*
- ☑ *Anxiety?*
- ☑ *Stress?*

Are you okay with them seeing or hearing any of that?

While you remain in this relationship, your children are at risk. Yes, they are in danger. What will you do when your abuser turns his aggression on your children? You wouldn't let them watch the movie, don't let them live it in real life.

If you're thinking about going back for the sake of the children, think again. I implore you to read this section over and over or join in the Facebook group conversation - <u>Broken to Blissful</u> Link: https://www.facebook.com/groups/brokentoblissful/

There is a real danger for your children in an abusive relationship. They are not passive witnesses. Children living with conflict and abuse will actively interpret, predict, and assess their future roles, assuming they are the cause of the abuse. They worry about the consequences and will try to protect their siblings and themselves from physical and emotional harm. In some cases, young children will attempt to physically stop their dad from beating mom and the child will be physically hurt. Your kids are also being used and abused by your abusive spouse. Your partner is abusing the children when he:

1. *Suggests a child's misbehaviour is the reason why he must be abusive. In other words, mom wouldn't get beaten if you were a good boy or girl*
2. *Encourages the children to abuse their mother by calling her demeaning names or laughing at her or dismissing her equality as a co-parent*
3. *Threatens violence against the children and/or pets*
4. *Talks inappropriately to the children about their mother's behaviour*

OUR CHILDREN

The Dangers Myth 2 Delivers On Them

At the time of my abusive relationship, my two beautiful girls were very young. He had given them a home, bikes, a backyard, and the ability to be free to play and grow. He also gave their mom bruises, nightmares, uncontrollable fits of crying, and fear. There were times when I couldn't function because I was depressed or anxious. They watched me go from having fun to shaking with fear just because he was on his way home. They took the brunt of my anxiety. I would yell, push them up to their rooms, or simply beg them to stay quiet and out of the way.

Imagine for one second what you would feel like watching a friend you care for being hurt. How would it make you feel? Would you want to step in and stop the pain? Run to her aid? Step in and make it all stop? Be honest. Now imagine you're a small child who has been told to respect their parents and do as they're told. You want to help mommy because she's hurting, but you're too small. Your voice is too little. You can't fight your father. In fact, you may get hit or yelled at too. Can you imagine their stress, their worry, their fear? That's the pain your children feel. Helplessness. Fear. Anxiety. Belittlement. Frustration, and all because you've been sold on the idea that you should stay for the kids.

I was caught up in the "look at all the beautiful things they have," and I didn't want to take that away from them. I felt I didn't have the right to deny them a home, stability, family vacations, and the other alleged perks of being a family... But here's the truth: they may have had their own rooms, but they were prisoners in them. They had room to play and lots of friends, but they had also learned to lie whenever asked why mommy had a black eye or why she cried all the time.

When I came to, after being choked almost to death, I could no longer deny I was living a lie. I knew I was harming my children. There was no end to the violence or the unhealthy environment. There was no excuse for staying.

I had no excuse to stay.

All children are harmed mentally and emotionally when they are kept in unhealthy, violent environments. They will repeat the cycle of abuse in their lives taking either the role of abuser or victim.

Young children grow up believing that it's normal and natural to be bullied, shouted at, harassed, and hit, in and out of relationships. When they begin exploring intimate relationships, if their new partner is aggressive or mean, they will use the patterns they learned in childhood to allow themselves to be abused. After all, that is what they saw, and it is now normalised in their minds.

That or the children become the abusers and use violence and bullying as a means to get the result they want. After all, that's what they were taught.

Break the Cycle

I know there is a cycle of abuse because I lived it. My parents were verbally abusive to one another. Equally, my father was physically violent with my mother. They too could tell tales of abuse filled childhoods. The scars of abuse they sustained as children continued in their adult life, delivering a daily verbal and emotional type of warfare. It also ushered in an age without pity. My parents, like those before them, practised judging others as a way to keep from examining themselves. It was easy for them to find fault outside of their marriage and just as easy for my sisters and me to learn to blame everyone but ourselves for how we felt, what we thought, and what we wanted in life and from others.

My parents were not the first generation in our chain of familial abuse. My mother's father was a brutal man. He beat my grandmother, his children, and even went to prison for sexually assaulting one of his teenage daughters. At the time, my grandmother had been institutionalised for a breakdown, and he believed it was in his right to press his wife's carnal duties on his eldest daughter. The scariest part of this horror is the number of men who still think this way.

My father grew up in a home where his mother was the abuser. Yup, his dad was a battered spouse. Abuse can come in any form, but it will only flourish when we allow it to exist without challenge. We all have regrets in life but don't let yours start with, "I should've, I could've, or I would've, if only I knew then what I know now."

By experience and without any example of something better, my mother and father carried forward what they learned at home. It's natural. As children, our parents are our teachers. If they are arguing and fighting and hurting each other, we learn that behaviour is acceptable. Even when we know better, learn better in school, or by the example of friends, the lesson is deeply rooted in our soul. It's a rinse and repeat pattern. The only way to stop abuse from spreading its poison through the next generations is for you to take a courageous step, Break the Cycle, leave your abusive relationship, and stay away.

Be The Change Your Children Deserve.

Break the cycle for them and teach them that violence, or any form of abuse, is not an acceptable part of their lives. Choose to teach them by example what healthy, loving relationships look like. Show them how to define and set boundaries and stand up for what they're learning is right. Let this be your legacy for this generation and the next one to come.

Right here, right now, get out the *Courage and Grace Workbook* and complete the exercises.

In the Eyes of a Child

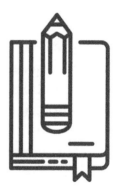

I'm not going to lie to you, the exercises in this section will be tough. They are designed to help you see the tragic, and unnecessary pain you are causing your children by staying with your abuser. The questions are real, raw, and honest. Open yourself up, get naked, listen to your heart, and gut voice. That's where the truth lives.

Custody, Visitation, and The Courts

There is huge anticipatory fear around leaving and leaving your children alone with your abuser because he has visitation. You may fear he will abuse them. You may fear he will use them in some way to get at you or otherwise cause them hardship and pain. And you could be right. But you may be wrong as well.

As with all fear-based anxiety, knowledge is paramount in moving forward. Get your facts straight. Don't think you know the outcome until you speak to a lawyer, a real lawyer, not that friend of a friend who's been there. It's great to have friends who want to help, especially your growing online community, but be warned. Everyone thinks they're an expert.

Even worse are the fakes and trolls who will try to mislead you or provide false information. It doesn't matter why they do this, just accept that when you need accurate legal advice, you need a real lawyer. All lawyers offer free consultations. Search online for family lawyers. Check out their websites, read their blogs, and take them up on their offer for a free consultation. Visit more than one so you have a consensus about what will happen. Any battle you may be facing is much easier to win when you are prepared.

Some Things to Consider

It is very rare for a biological parent to be denied some level of access to their children. To calm your fear, be prepared. Keep detailed notes about what has happened in the home, to you, and to your kids. Keep your journal too. Make sure you have written down what you desire and what your compromises will be. You may be called in court to present facts and details that you are trying hard to forget. Your best defence is to write it all down now. Keep records of everything and be prepared to share those painful details in court.

Your desire and your compromise are unique, and each needs to be expressed in extreme detail. Dates, times, money, holidays, vacations, extended family visits, schools, moving to a new town, city or country, recreation, sports, concerts—every detail should be recorded! Doing this creates a clear picture of your boundaries—what's acceptable and what isn't.

Now you're prepared to discuss, meditate, or go to full trial. You are well positioned to negotiate the terms acceptable to you and the very best for your kids.

His New Special Friend

Yup, this will happen. Your ex will start dating. In my case, his new girlfriend was already on the scene. This will bring up a variety of strong, natural emotions, including, *Keep that bitch away from my children!* Well, you may feel this way, and it can be very painful to watch your children meeting a new potential step-mom every few months, but there is nothing you can do about it. That's the truth.

Have a private response to the new special friend and a public one. Your private response can be filled with nasty commentary meant for your ears only. Journal your feelings. Get them out because you do not want to express your negative private feelings about the new friend in front of your children. Never. Not once. Not ever.

The failure of your marriage is not about her. It's about you accepting that *he* is an abuser. In fact, you may want to feel sorry for her. She's in the same place you were when you fell for him and his lies and manipulations. When it comes to her, keep your feelings to yourself. Telling family or friends is dangerous because words can come back to haunt you. Keep it private. Between you and only you, and on the days it hurts too much, remember, she's right where you once were, on the verge of falling into his trap. He may try to make you think he treats her differently, that she's somehow deserving of the love he withheld from you. Don't believe it. Don't even go there.

What Your Kids See, They Repeat!

MYTH THREE

I Have No Money, No Friends, No Family...

This was my greatest hardship. I remember wondering and worrying about who would help me. How would I get moved back to the city where my family lived? How would I get moved back to the city where I had grown up? How would the girls react to starting a new school? Where the hell was I going to get the money?

I didn't work. I let *him* take that from me. He promised to care for us if I would become a full-time wife and mother. It was offered as a perk or reward but was actually a means of control. Once I no longer had a job, I no longer had my own money. Now I had to ask for every extra penny over and above the meagre household budget. A budget set by him as he was the only breadwinner. Suddenly I wasn't an adult to be included in the discussion of household finances, I was a child being schooled by the master of our home. I was required to show receipts for groceries and other personal necessities. When school trips came up, or pizza day, or anytime I needed extra money, it was a difficult conversation. One that I stressed over every time. Somehow, giving up my job, even though it was at his urging, reduced my status from partner to a dependent unworthy of a voice in the financial conversation.

Where was I going to get the money?

I needed to move a long distance. I needed a place to stay with my two children. And I needed cash for food and transportation.

On top of my feelings of sorrow and anger, there was a huge helping of embarrassment. I was beating myself up, repeating over and over that I let this happen and I should have known better. The shame we feel can stop us from reaching out to friends and family. I vividly remember sitting with the phone in my hand, shaking, and thinking, *What will my sister say to me when I call? How will I possibly explain the shit that has happened?* I cried because I was mortified to tell her my story.

Remember, we often put on a show for outsiders so when it comes time to ask for help, we think we need to swallow our pride and step into our embarrassment. There is nothing to apologise for or feel ashamed about. Your life is not defined by what he did to you. This is your story now. Your only job is to own it, as ugly and horrible as it may feel in the moment.

Pick up the phone and ask!

I called several people, family, and friends, and although they were sympathetic, the majority did not want to get involved. You will hear that so many times in your quest for help. Don't quit after the first or second or third try.

Keep going. Keep asking. Keep phoning.

Remember too that you have been maintaining the illusion of a perfect relationship for so long, many friends and family will want to defend the fiction you invented about your abuser. Don't worry, in time most, if not all, will accept the truth. Still, you can't wait for them to come around. Find your supporters.

I found my one and only ally in a cousin who owned a very tiny house in the core of the city. I was quite surprised because she had very little space but was willing to offer my girls and me some form of accommodation. Okay, it was a furnace room but here's the great part about the furnace room – it was mine, and he was not there. Period!

It Was My Palace and Healing Sanctuary.

Keep your focus on getting out, staying out, and moving on. That's more important than fixating on the type or size of accommodation you will temporarily land in. It's a building block to your future. Don't shun any offers of assistance. It's just a step, one small step forward. Having my accommodation issues resolved was a great feeling, as you can imagine, but I'm sure you're asking yourself about the money. Yes, money is real, and there is a certain amount that we need. It's called personal financial responsibility.

One of the biggest obstacles women have when it comes to leaving is a lack of money. They are often cut off from all the financial decisions in the household and have no direct access to saving or cash. You want to leave your abusive relationship desperately, but you start thinking about all the things you will have to do. And all of it seems to take a huge amount of cash. The lack of money becomes a tremendous obstacle. It's supposed to be a hurdle. After all, it's one of the tools he used to keep you trapped. Money can be that one obstacle which seems insurmountable, but it's not.

I remember it well. The cold sweats, questioning how I would provide a home for my children? Food? Clothing? My husband had lured me into financial dependency, begging me to quit my job with stories of how he would love to support me so I could be a full-time mom to my girls. I fell for it. The outcome: I had no access to bank accounts, bank cards, or credit cards. The household spending was in cash, and receipts and change were accounted for daily.

Saving a few dollars each week was difficult, but I did manage to do it. I didn't save a lot, but it was enough to offer to pay for some groceries when I landed in my cousin's furnace room. And that little bit made me feel good about myself. And I needed that.

I know from personal experience that money can be one of the biggest obstacles to getting out and staying out of an abusive relationship.

There are resources available, and I highly recommend that you find and receive all the help you can muster. You will build strength and resilience when you feel that you can manage your day-to-day finances and maintain a home for your kids. Your thoughts of running back will lessen, and you will begin to relax and enjoy the new life that you are creating.

Search for support from Family Services, Community Services, Welfare, Income Assistance, and more. Use the programs out there. They were created by men and women who know this can happen to anyone and that no one deserves to be abused.

Access all the government and social services that you can find. Don't be embarrassed. You're on a path to righting your life, and whether he likes it or not, our society is prepared to take action to help you stay away and get back on your feet.

This is not where your journey will end. It's just a step on the path back to the real you. Take the help, use it as a step up, to start over, and begin to take complete responsibility for your new life for yourself and your kids.

Right here, right now, get out the *Courage and Grace Workbook* and complete the exercise...

What Resources Are Available?

Courage and Grace

Chapter Four

MOVING OUT OF THE VICTIM'HOOD

"As I walked out the door toward the gate that would lead to my freedom, I knew that if I didn't leave my bitterness and hatred behind, I would STILL be in prison."
                                                    Nelson Mandela

One beautiful Autumn day I ran into a family friend I had not seen in over a decade. We were so excited for the random meeting that we decided to have lunch and catch up. Her first question was, "What's been going on in your life?" And that question gave me the opening to begin to tell my amazing victim story. I told her about the cheating, the violence, the furnace room, the sorrow and the anger. She sat in silence and drank her coffee and I remember thinking she should be saying something, offering me condolences, or shaking her head in horror at my victim story. But she didn't. Instead, she said this: "Susan, that is a fucking boring story. Time to write a new happy story."

Courage and Grace

I was so pissed off!

How dare she say that to me? I was a victim of domestic violence. I deserved to be treated with extreme kindness. I could tell my story whenever I felt like it and I deserved sympathy. Period. Or so I thought.

I left the restaurant and decided I never wanted to see her again. But she had planted a seed. Was I wallowing in my victim story? Was I avoiding healing and letting go?

Was I comfortable in my victim space?

I realised that to create a happy story for myself and my girls. I had to take control of my life and accept responsibility for my actions. Period. No excuses.

During my darkest moments, I could not see colours other than black, grey and red. Red for revenge. That colour popped when I thought about him and my situation and how he was responsible for the fact that my life was now shit.

The rest of the time I saw only black and grey. There was no colour in my thoughts. My imagination and my future looked very dreary, uncreative and bland at best. Black and grey are the colours of hopelessness and depression. It's the palette of a victim.

I walked through my days not able to see anything good or bright or hopeful in my future. I wanted to. I sat sometimes and tried with all my heart to imagine a happy future that I had created for myself and my kids. But the truth was my victim was keeping me trapped in the black and grey world. Me and victim, we were simpatico, and it was easy to stay there. Comfortable. Relaxing. No work required.

Staying a victim and living a victim's life allowed me to avoid any personal responsibility for what I was doing, where I was going, or what I wanted in my future. I could simply say, well, "I'm a victim of domestic violence," and" if it weren't for that I would definitely be an astronaut but how can I? Horrible things happened to me, and I'm going to hang on to those terrible events for dear life! If I never let go, I can't reach out and grab my chance to be an astronaut. I can't, and it's not my fault!"

That's the way victim's think and go through their life, but the newly planted seed of writing a new happy story was beginning to sprout. Could it be possible for me to be happy? Healthy? Productive? Could I be a good role model to my daughters? Could I go back to school? Could I learn to drive and do all the things he said I was too stupid to do? Was that possible for me?

Don't be defined by your victim experience.

Where to begin and how to do it was a complete mystery but I felt compelled to move forward. It was time to let go of my brutal assault, to forgive, to mend my brokenness, and embrace all the possibilities. My potential was waiting to be discovered. I learned support for domestic violence survivors is passive and reliant on repeated telling of your victim story. It doesn't encourage active pursuit of your dreams, goals, joys, and happiness.

As I struggled with the emotions of fear, sadness, and guilt, and stood on the precipice of alcoholism, I had a profound moment of clarity–the system wasn't working for me. It was making me depressed and keeping me in the past. It was killing my spirit, denying me happiness, and it was slowing my progress.

Something was missing.

I stepped away from the system and went on a solo journey of self-discovery, and I stumbled upon something incredible. I discovered the importance of celebrating my successes and forging new positive connections while facing my challenges head-on. I learned how to do this by setting goals and planning.

What I needed then and what we all seek, is the active support that helps us move forward, build strength, resilience, confidence, and self-reliance. I couldn't find that within the system, so I created my own. One that focuses on Joy, Gratitude, and Success, and now I'm sharing it with you.

Right here, right now, get out the *Courage and Grace Workbook* and complete the exercise…

Top 10 Stories You've Told Yourself that Hold You Back?

BANISH YOUR LIES

"I believe if you just stand up and go, life will open up for you."
Tina Turner

I vividly remember all the lies I told myself when I thought about leaving my abuser. I would come up with so much bullshit, I would end up in a state of panic. And panic led me to stay. He had convinced me I was a complete idiot who would never survive without him.

I would have a moment of strength and shout screw you, I can, and will leave and make it on my own. And then I would wither on the vine and think, *you know he's probably right, I'll die without him.*

I made excuses for his behaviour and worked very hard to believe my own bullshit. The stories I created were my excuses to stay in the relationship. It was so easy to tell myself I can't leave just because he was in a bad mood that day. I can't leave, I have to think of the kids, and despite his outbursts, he's a good dad.

Every one of my stories fed into my Can't's.

If right now, you are still living in a shitty, manipulative relationship and you say you want to leave, what's stopping you? Are you committed to leaving? Are you preparing to move mountains and sling burgers if that's what it takes? Or perhaps you're on the other side of the door and you've left your abuser but you still think going back would solve your problems. Or that if you go back this time, he will change, and the relationship will be happy and stable. Is that what you've been telling yourself?

What is it you imagine you can't do outside the relationship? What is it you're not willing to sacrifice to live a better, happier, healthier life?

In other words, what are the excuses you're telling yourself?

There are lies we tell ourselves every day, and they offer protection from our vulnerability and our fear of change. We feel protected within the cocoon of our cant's. It's a very comforting feeling just to say I can't do that, or I could never cope with that, or my children can't face that.

All our lies start with "Can't," "Could not," "Never," "Not a chance," and "No." The pattern is endless, but the result is the same:

You're stuck in a holding pattern.

"Can't," makes us powerless in our lives and allows us to be victims. We revert to can't because our instinct is to want assurances that it will work before we go after the changes we desire or make any big move. Technically, this is known as Anticipatory Fear.

Right here, right now, get out the *Courage and Grace Workbook* and complete the exercise...

Get Real and Be Honest

Anticipatory Fear

"Everything you've ever wanted is on the other side of fear."
George Addair

I remember sitting in my big house, thinking about leaving him. The spiral of fearful thoughts that took over my mind was terrifying. One leads to another that led to the next. It was vibrant and felt so real. I was shaking in terror and all because of anticipatory fear. It works on your fear of the unknown and it embellishes any small bit of anxiety you may be experiencing. Actually, it blows everything way the fuck out of proportion.

As your mind bends the truth and grows the fear, you revert back to staying because that seems so much better than leaving. It's your mind playing mind games with you.

The Game Goes Like This...

You: That's it, I'm leaving him. I deserve better!

Your mind: Where will you go? How will you feed your children? You have no job. No skills. You're stupid, remember? He said so.

You a little weaker: I'll find a job somewhere, and maybe my parents will let me stay for a bit.

Mind laughing and judging: You're going to run to your parents and uproot your kids just because he got a little angry last night? Looser!

Reading the dialogue, you can clearly see how your voice becomes weaker, you begin to fold inside, feeling another part of you disappear. Now more timid, as your mind gives you examples of the unknown. You continue to create questions that make you feel weaker, and as your resolve weakens, the anticipation and fear of the unknown overtake your logic and your strength.

It's okay to fail the first time the thought of leaving hits you. If you are staying in an abusive relationship because you think you can't leave or thrive on your own, it's simply not true.

Right here, right now, get out the Courage and Grace Workbook and complete the exercise...

What Will Happen If You...

Is it possible to be overwhelmed by all the things you never imagined needing to do? Of course, you don't *Want* to move. Of course, you don't *Want* to change jobs. Of course, you don't *Want* to put the kids in a new school.

There are a lot of things we don't want to do in life but we are adults, and that means we have responsibilities to our community, our family, our children, and first and foremost to ourselves. Be honest with yourself. Are you using your Cant's as reasons why you Won't?

It's Time, Start Changing Your Won't's to I Will!

Being a Blissful Thriver is all about breaking down and throwing away our excuses. It's about taking responsibility for outcomes and making sure that we are living a life we truly desire and love. Massive shifts happen when you accept responsibility for your choices and your life. Yes, you are 100% responsible for the quality of your life.

Your life is about you!

Activate and Embrace Your Blissful Thriver

We've all watched the Wizard of Oz. There is a powerful and wise lesson given to Dorothy by Glinda the Good Witch, when she tells Dorothy, "You had the power all along."

If you're in an abusive relationship, you have the power to change your life. You have the power to walk away. You have the power to create a life of true peace. And you have the power to keep moving, keep growing and keep discovering the real you as you grow and change.

You have the power... Period!

Whenever you think, *Why?* You're setting a limit for yourself. When you change your thinking to, *How?* You open up your mind to solutions and ways to solve your problem. Start paying attention to how often you get stuck thinking I *don't know how* and start considering *how do I?* Courage is not about living without fear; it's about feeling the fear and taking action anyway.

The questions we ask ourselves can drastically influence our state, our life, our happiness, and our ability to create our dream life. There is a danger in fixating on the wrong questions because it can keep you locked in your victim story and in some cases, attached to your abuser.

Questions that begin with "Why" are rhetorical and can not be adequately answered. They keep you motionless. Healing from an abusive relationship requires forward momentum. You've got to move to heal. Why questions do not have the power to move you in any direction. Consider them paralysing.

Questions with the Power to Move You Forward

Instead of asking, "Why is my heart broken?" Ask yourself, **"What can I do to heal my heart?"**

Instead of asking, "Why can't I be happy?" Ask yourself, "What can I do to change my situation and start feeling happy?"

And if you're asking, "Why does my life suck?" Start asking **"What can I do to change my life?"**

Asking quality questions creates a quality life…and the more quality questions you ask, the more likely you are to create an outstanding life. It's up to you to be courageous and take the first graceful step. Your freedom, peace, and happiness are waiting for you.

Continuing a negative internal dialogue, and all the "Why's" can easily trap you in a spiral of self-fulfilling prophecy. This is the most dangerous aspect at the core of your limiting beliefs. Our minds are hot-wired to deliver the things we believe we deserve. If you have been convinced by your abuser, family, friends, society, etc., that you are stupid, your heart-mind-and-soul will work night and day to make that real.

Imagine for a moment that you have a clone, someone who looks just like you, who works in the background to do all those little things you never have time to do. Your wish is her command, and the great part is, you don't have to tell your clone what to do. After all, she's you and intuitively knows what you need. You're sending her signals all day, and , all night when you sleep and your subconscious mind is hard at work trying to sort out your thoughts and work to make your life match your vision. Yes, your clone will be up all night trying to figure out how to get you what you've been asking for and what you're dreaming of.

Now imagine it's a bright new day and you've spent all your previous night telling yourself, and your clone, "I'm stupid." While you slept, she worked hard to make that true. After all, it's what you want, right? The first thing you notice when you wake is you forgot to set your alarm. As you race through getting the kids up, dressed, fed, and off to school, you keep repeating your mantra, "I'm stupid." As your day progresses so too are your mistakes. Don't worry about looking stupid; your clone is making sure it happens all day long. You mix up names, sound confused, and miss appointments, all the while reinforcing your command to your clone to make sure you look, act, and sound like whatever it is you think stupid is.

At the end of the day you fall into bed a disaster of your own making, even more convinced of those self-deprecating lies. Now imagine if you told yourself, your mind, and your clone, "I'm smart and resourceful." I know that sounds like a lie at first, especially if you have been told, repeatedly told, you're not smart or capable. Don't worry, it's just like telling yourself you're stupid. Your clone knows it may be in new territory, but she's programmed to help you achieve exactly what you want. So, telling yourself that you are all the things you want to be is like having a Genie grant you unlimited wishes. Your mind wants you to be what you imagine. Let your clone work it out and not in the negative. You don't need those old lies no matter how deeply embedded.

Another way to consider your core belief is to label the parts of your spirit and personality. Are you competitive or were you a competitive girl? Women are trained to believe we are not competitive. It's a lie. We are just as competitive as guys. It's in our DNA. After all, your stone-age ancestor was not the one who said, "You go first," when the sabre tooth tiger was chasing her and the other women from her village. No! Your ancestor was one of the women who learned to survive. She was either the fastest runner, leading the escapees, or the fighter who miraculously survived the attack. We, like our mom and her mom before her, have been lied to. The demure lady who stands by her man is a fiction. The truth is, you are made of tougher stuff and to accept that truth you may want to connect with your competitive side, the Prover inside of you.

Meet Your Prover

Your Prover is another way of defining your subconscious mind. It's the fight that kept you alive and got you and your kids out. It's that determined voice that keeps you away from him even when everyone says go back. It's the internal voice of strength and determination, but the Prover inside of you also has a significant weakness. She doesn't know what's good for you and what isn't. She's programmed to react to your beliefs. If you believe you need to stand up and fight the system, she'll be your champion, standing tall and taking on the man. If your belief system is riddled with lies and negative thoughts on your own abilities, she will work tirelessly to prove them to be true. Like your clone, she reacts to prove what you genuinely believe.

If you believe you are smart, the Prover inside of you will prove that to be true. If you tell yourself, "I'm stronger than they know," your Prover will make that true too. That's how your belief system works. If you think and tell yourself that you will never be able to live without your abuser and be successful on your own, your prover will step forward and show you how right you are. You'll find evidence everywhere. Your negative thoughts and negative self-talk are your limiting beliefs, and they are undermining your potential.

Still not sure what your beliefs are, ask yourself if any of the following sound familiar?

- ☑ *I couldn't...*
- ☑ *I can't figure it out...*
- ☑ *I can't raise the money...*
- ☑ *I can't go it alone...*
- ☑ *I'll never be able to do it...*
- ☑ *I'll never get the money...*

Are you surprised to see just how universal some of our limiting beliefs are? Limiting beliefs are not reasons for your situation. When you repeat these negative and false beliefs, you stop yourself from moving forward. You trick yourself into believing you are not capable or worthy of creating your own personal happiness. These negative and limiting beliefs create doubt and influence your behaviour. And they are what he uses against you.

The truth is we lie to ourselves every day. That's not a bad thing. Some days it's a simple lie to coax ourselves out of bed. When these lies help us up, they can become the foundation for new and positive beliefs. If you think, this sounds like Law of Attraction hooey, I want you to take a moment and imagine the scales of justice. I'm not talking about the legal system but the statue of Lady Justice, blindfolded to hear only the truth and holding up an old-fashioned weight scale to indicate the equal weight of all the facts. I want you to place any of your limiting beliefs on one side of the scale. Imagine it being heavily weighted down will all the instances you have allowed your negative beliefs to be renewed or reinforced. Now, on the other side, place your delicate new belief. See how the old belief heavily weighs the scale in that direction? Now if you think that gives the bad stuff credence, think again. It's simply a measure of how much you need to add weight to your new belief. As you do, and your positive beliefs begin to take on weight, the negative will break down quickly, getting lighter and lighter until weightless. That's when your new positive belief will be fully anchored. Once anchored your mind, your Prover and you will know it to be true.

Negative Beliefs Are Nothing but the Bad Lies We Choose or Were Told to Accept

Don't beat yourself up if you find you have been perpetuating the lies that held you back. We didn't start out in life saying mean limiting things to ourselves. People did. People in authority did. People we trusted and they did because it was what they were taught. The same limits you were given, were given to your mother, and her mother before that. You have a choice about these lies. You can continue to accept them, and if you do, you will by your example, transfer the same limiting beliefs to your kids.

Accepting these lies is easy. They give us permission to stay stuck in our painful and dangerous situation. After all, you're not going to go looking at apartments if you're already telling yourself, "I can't afford to move." Even if your Prover is shouting at the page, insisting she has no limiting beliefs, we do.

How can that be? You got out, that's great. Great Job! You got out, but moving from the role of the abused spouse to the victim'hood is only a step. One small step in a series of small steps. You don't have to tiptoe from abuse. Remember, your ancestor didn't waste any time grabbing the kids and running for her life from the sabretooth tiger, why should you?

Leaving is powerful. Walking out that door and boldly proclaiming "Enough of that shit, and I'm worth so much more," is courageous. Your first steps are critical. They begin the journey of healing but there's a danger up ahead, and that's getting stuck in the Victim'hood.

You've left him, but it is easy to play the role of the victim. To believe that you are unworthy, incapable and that this is as good as it gets. Sticking yourself in victim'hood is bullshit. You were a victim while the abuse was happening. Once you leave, you are a survivor, and once you accept responsibility for your happiness and your life, you liberate your Blissful Thriver.

> *The Recovery Industry, as I like to call it, is notorious for perpetuating the victim mentality with a dash of you're a survivor. There is a reluctance to encourage survivors to look inside themselves to heal the gaping wound causing them to repeatedly attract nasty, ugly human beings into their lives.*
>
> *In the Industry, asking survivors to heal themselves, let go, and move on is commonly known as Victim Blaming. This is crap.*

I call Bullshit!

You aren't being blamed for anything. You are being asked to honestly evaluate your past hurts, limiting beliefs, and low self-worth issues so you can heal, grow and radiate self-love. Asking you to liberate yourself from your limiting beliefs and sparkle in your authentic bright light is not victim blaming.

It is Freedom. It's Power. *It's You, Reclaiming You.* Plain and Simple.

Right here, right now, get out the *Courage and Grace Workbook* and complete the exercise...

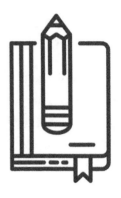

**Taking Action
with
I Am, I Can, & I Will**

The Anatomy of a Limiting Belief

Limiting beliefs are rooted in our word choices and these, in turn, fuel our fear-based thinking and anxiety. Remember that ancient ancestor? She knew fear, and she knew how to turn that fear into power. In our example, she knew to run for her life until she could find a safe refuge for her and her kids. She would have needed to hunt and gather for her family and teach her children all her skills just to survive.

We are all scared of starting over but examining your internal language will help you separate the facts from the fear. The first step in challenging your limiting beliefs begins by listening to the tell-tale presuppositions (A supposition is a belief, where a presupposition is an assumption based on some pre-existing limit – often a limiting belief that has nothing to do with you).

Here Are A few Examples

I can't...

I shouldn't...

If only...

Yeah, but...

No...

I'm not like (them, you, someone who succeeded)...

None of these sentence openings will move you in the direction you want to go. They all assume you are not capable of change. They will not lead you on a journey of healing. They will keep you stuck in a loop of anticipatory fear and self-doubt. If you begin any discussion or planning with I **Can't**, you are firmly and unequivocally telling your brain and your heart you **Won't**.

Can't Means Won't

Your first job in changing your belief system is accepting you can and you will. Maybe you don't know how, yet, but saying "You can," allows a transformation to begin deep within you. It tells your mind to figure it out. It gives you permission to be the smart, resourceful woman you are, and opens you to the answers and opportunities all around us.

"You had the power all along."
Glinda, the Good Witch

Turning Limiting Beliefs into Validating Beliefs

You have a choice. You can talk to yourself in a limiting, negative way, and give away your hope and power before you even start. Or, you can speak to yourself with powerful validating, empowering, and confidence-building words.

Validating beliefs being with:

I Am—I Can—I Will

Adopt the attitude of *The Little Engine that Could*. He simply said "I think I can, I think I can," and when the time came, he did, because he had already empowered himself to succeed.

Even when you are having trouble believing in the language that will move you forward, remember your clone, your Prover, that subconscious helper. She's working all night to make your beliefs your reality. Adopting positive, helpful affirmations, described using validating language, is one fantastic way to foster and imprint your new supportive beliefs.

I did it, and I know you can too!

Validating language and beliefs are quickly fostered through the creation and daily use of positive affirmations. Affirmations love the three "P's" – **present tense, personal**, and **positive**. Write as many as you need and read them aloud every morning and every night right before bed. Yes, add this practice to writing in your gratitude journal. You should recite your affirmations daily, ideally before bed and first thing in the morning. Don't have time? Pin your affirmations to the outside of the bathroom shower glass and recite them while you shower. You can read your affirmations while you're on the bus, in the subway, or waiting to pick up the kids from practice. When it's important, you find the time.

As your life and circumstances change, your affirmations will change to reflect your new situation. Use your affirmations to combat self-doubt whenever it creeps in. Repeat, repeat, and repeat again to push the negative self-talk away. It takes time to overcome years and sometimes generations of limiting beliefs. The good news is it won't take nearly as long to replace these old limits with your new personal empowerments.

Whenever you're in doubt, close your eyes and remember the scales of justice. Except, you're holding them up, and you are free to put your thumb on the scale and tip things in your favour. As a matter of fact, imagining those old negative beliefs, even piled sky high, flaking apart right before your eyes and blowing away. You can have fun with the mental image of self-empowerment. All that old baggage may look intimidating. Don't let it. Imagine those scales of justice are completely in your control. With a simple poke, allow yourself to witness your negative beliefs disintegrate right before your eyes.

Affirmations are personal and powerful so go ahead and pile them on your new scales of justice and build your positive mindset. When I began my solo healing journey, I found the strength and the resolve to keep going when I began writing down all the things I was determined to accomplish. As I did, I became freer to describe a more ideal vision of my future. I was filling in the colour, inviting opportunities and considering all sorts of dreams and paths to follow. I admitted on paper that I was capable, smart, and open to great change. I dismissed the worries of how and focused on what I wanted me to be and what I wanted for my life.

To successfully transform your validating language, you must focus on you and you alone. What about the kids, you ask? When you open yourself to change, to be who you were meant to be, you open a whole new world for your children. Your new and improving opportunities become their opportunities too.

These are my personal daily affirmations. Please use them if they speak to you or use them as examples of all you can create for yourself.

Example Positive Affirmations

- ☑ *I am self-reliant*
- ☑ *I live my life my way*
- ☑ *I am a good role model to my kids*
- ☑ *I am happy and successful*
- ☑ *I am courageous*
- ☑ *I am worthy*
- ☑ *I can overcome any challenge*
- ☑ *I am continually moving forward and achieving my goals*

Self-confidence is the memory of success. Each goal you achieve or small step that you take is worthy of celebration. And every time you celebrate your success, you find yourself stepping fully into self-love and confidence in all areas of your life.

Right here, right now, get out the Courage and Grace Workbook and complete the exercise...

7-Step Limiting Belief

Taking Action

The exercises you have already completed help to define where you are now, where you want to be, and most importantly how you're going to get there.

You have already written your plan. It's right here in the pages of your Workbook and Journal. Each step to move you forward, help you let go, and write your new life's chapter is clear. Take the time to reflect on what you've written, and you'll find your courage and your grace. You have successfully eliminated your excuses, and now it's time to take consistent, focused action toward the big, juicy goal you set in your Workbook.

Open your Workbook to the section titled...

My Fat Juicy Life!

This is what you wrote before you even started all your self-care, self-love, and change work.

Now go Make it a Reality.

Decide What You Want
Visualise it.
Make a Freaking Plan
Then... Work on it—Every—Single—Day

Your story is so much more than what happened to you. I got all caught up in my victim story. It was comfortable there. I could talk about it. I could let it comfort me. I could let it determine how I acted. My life made sense. I hung onto my story because I was afraid to let it go. Letting go felt like I would fall into a dark abyss filled with nothing and no-one. I was terrified of the emptiness I imagined would exist after letting my story go.

You keep your story because it's safe. As long as you tell that story, you don't have to step out of your comfort zone and face your fears. It's easy to get stuck, and it takes a great deal of courage to get un-stuck.

It Takes Dedication, Determination and Desire to Live with Freedom, Peace, and Happiness

When I decided to let go of my victim story and the past hurts, I walked into my great adventure. One that keeps growing and improving. I realised something else too. My story had taught me so much about what I actually wanted in my life, what I would and would no longer accept and who I would embrace on my new journey.

Consciously deciding to let my past go, was the most terrifying and rewarding experience rolled together into one! I am so happy I stepped out of my past, healed, and stepped into my brilliant present. Since leaving my abuser and ditching my victim story, I have blossomed through self-love, defining my beliefs and respecting my values, while learning and living with joy and playfulness. I have accomplished all the things he said I was too dumb to do—learning to drive, a university education with honours, self-employment, travel, and writing.

I have found true and respectful love and partnership. The kind of love where we grow together and change with the flow of life. There is no rigidity. We live and laugh in the present and look forward to the future. Laughter is an everyday occurrence. But my greatest achievement is that I honour me and who I am. My quirks, my body, and my mind are unique, and I love that about me.

In a very odd way, I thank him for the experience because I learned how to be me, how to love me, and how to be comfortable alone in my own skin.

Let yourself know this is only a chapter and now it's time to turn the page and move on.

Your big, bold, blissful story is waiting to be written and lived, but it's up to you. It's your story, you're the author, and it's as simple as turning the page and starting with you!

Are You Ready to Move Forward and Create Your Big, Bold, Joy-Filled Life?

Are you ready? YES?????

If you can honestly say, "I Am Ready, Willing, and Able," start here:

Imagine it's a year from today, and I'm calling you. What will you tell me about all the great stuff happening in your life? I want to hear about your courage. I want to hear about your blissful life. I want to hear about you finding your grace. I really do! Go to the website or send me an email right now and book a date and time to Skype with me in a year from now. This is my challenge to you. I want you to tell me all about finding your courage and your grace.

You're so ready to get blissful, grow wings, and fly.

XO,

Susan

Self-Confidence Is the Memory of Success.

Book your call now. I'm waiting to hear from you.

http://www.susanball.ca

Writing Your Dream Life

What You Need to Hear, See, and Feel to Move Towards Your Blissful Life

A blissful life is right there in front of you. To get there, you have to let go of fear, anger, sorrow, bitterness and blame.

Here's a story I love to use to demonstrate letting go:

Two Buddhist monks are returning to their monastery during the rainy season. They reach a swollen river and in front of them is an extremely beautiful lady in a delicate silk kimono. She is distressed because she is unable to cross the river by herself.

The older monk scoops her up, carries her safely to the other side, then continues in silence with the younger monk at his side.

Five hours later, as the two monks reach their destination, the younger monk, literally fuming, bursts out, "How could you do it? You touched a woman; you know we're not allowed to do that!"

The older monk replied, "I put her down five hours ago, but you are still carrying her with you!"

Letting go will open your life to all the fabulous possibilities waiting for you to embrace. Letting go requires forgiveness and acceptance. Accept that what has happened to you was one chapter and only one part of your life. Forgive yourself. You were tricked.

When we accept and forgive, we set ourselves free and get to reclaim that energy for ourselves.

Wisdom Whisper

What you don't HEAL, you CARRY
What you CARRY, needs FEEDING
What you FEED, Gets BIGGER
What gets BIGGER, needs YOUR ATTENTION
What needs your ATTENTION, needs HEALING
What is HEALED, can GO AWAY
What GOES AWAY, can be REPLACED
Now the ORIGINAL can BE SEEN

Resources

Downloads: http://www.susanball.ca/just-for-you/

Order the book, workbook, and Journal from Amazon:

https://www.amazon.com/Susan-Ball/e/B01MF5NKNC/

Join the Facebook Group: Broken to Blissful

https://www.facebook.com/groups/brokentoblissful/

Reserve your VIP spot: http://www.susanball.ca/be-my-v-i-p/

Appendix A

BROKEN TO BLISSFUL FOUNDATIONAL TOOLKIT

The healing journey you're on needs a solid foundation to build confidence, joy, courage, peace, and happiness. These five tools are meant to be soothing, challenging, and forward focused. They are specifically written to help you disassociate from your abuse and create space in your heart, soul, and mind for healing.

As you move along your path creating, doing, and growing, you will use these foundational tools daily with one exception: RaW or the Rage and Weep exercises.

As you focus on building joy, achieving your new goals and celebrating your successes, your moments of RaW will lessen. Make sure you celebrate how your emotional state is recovering and moving from Broken to Blissful. That's worthy of a huge, dancing, smiling, laughing and joyful celebration.

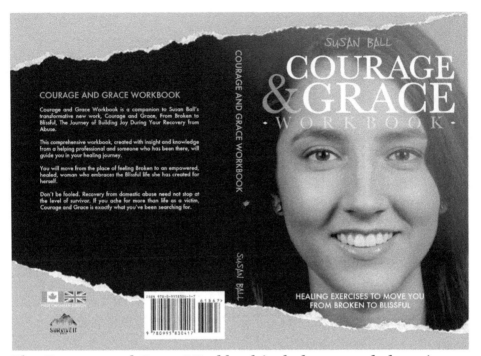

The *Courage and Grace Workbook* includes expanded versions of the Foundational Toolkit exercises. You can download the workbook from your retailer or my website: www.susanball.ca

Your Foundational Toolkit

1. *Name IT*
2. *RaW: Rage and Weep*
3. *Breathing Exercise*
4. *Disconnecting & Reconnecting with Small Joyful Things*
5. *Writing from the Heart Journal Prompts*

In addition to your *Courage and Grace Workbook*, I recommend you purchase a Journal for writing and reflection. (You may order the *Courage and Grace Freedom Journal* from your book retailer. Or visit Susan's website for more information: http://www.susanball.ca)

Make your time journaling special. Choose a quiet place and time to write. Add a nice cup of tea, coffee, or a glass of wine. Use a beautiful pen in a fun colour and make sure there are no distractions, technological, or human disruptions. Freely write. Don't worry about grammar or spelling. Just write from your heart. Let your thoughts and feelings flow onto the page. Free your voice and your life through your writing.

GETTING STARTED WITH WRITING PROMPTS

Opening your journal and finding a blank page staring back at you can feel overwhelming and you may be tempted to give up. Don't! I want you to succeed, and I know you can.

To help, I've provided some writing prompts to get you started:

Today I'm grateful for...

Today I showed courage when I...

Today I am worthy of...

Today I know I am healing and I know I can...

Today I will create... And I will step gracefully into...

NAME IT!

You're Asking Yourself What the Hell Is Name IT!

It Sounds Like a Game Show from The 1970s.
Cue The Music!

In reality, this is your release from the hurt, from the pain, from reliving it over and over again. This is you freeing your life from the shackles of your abusive relationship.

This was a life-changing discovery for me in my personal journey.

You want to name your abusive experience. You need to give what happened to you a name or a word or a phrase. Why? It depersonalises what happened to you. It moves you away from the person who hurt you. It insulates you from re-experiencing your abuse and limits your abuser's place to a mere reference point in your life's timeline.

"You have no power over me."
Sarah, Labyrinth, 1986

I named mine "The Incident" and it now lives comfortably without reference to the man. I have divided the experience into two reference points:

Before the Incident and After the Incident.

Let's Name IT!

You can use any reference that is comfortable and removes the person. For example, My Moment, My Epiphany, That One Time, The Circus.

In your Workbook or *your Courage and Grace Freedom Journal*, write out the name you want to use to refer to your period of abuse. You're not naming your abuser. He has no power here. This is what you will forever call that specific period in your life.

I name, IT...

Now you have a name for IT. When you're asked any questions, you can simply ask, "Are you referring to (say the name you have given the incident)," to describe that period. Immediately, you will begin disassociating from the person who caused the trauma.

Today, my friends and family easily refer to "The Incident" when they're talking to me or asking questions. It has become part of our language and holds no power over me.

Rage and Weep Exercise

RaW™

Your heart needs to weep and your mind needs to rage so you can heal. You won't do one or the other. You will Rage & Weep at the same time. Your tears will be fierce, and the pain in your heart will be real. It hurts.

Your mind struggles to understand. The noise and chatter going on is confusing and keeps you wondering *what if*? But every time you let your RaW emotions come out, your heart heals just a bit, and you find renewed strength and courage to move forward. The chatter lessens, and clarity begins to appear.

At my lowest point, sitting on my bed in my friend's furnace room, I believed I had to be stoic. To show that I was tough and wasn't going to let the end of an abusive relationship break me down into a weeping puddle.

I was wrong, and it almost killed me.

Holding in your RaW emotions keeps you living in the past. It keeps you tied to your victim story. It suppresses your future and deadens your present. Take time to get naked and RaW.

Step One

Today I WEPT, and That's Okay

Be honest and write down all the reasons you were weeping. Express the why, and the steps you have taken to move forward, to heal your wound. What was I crying for? Lost Love? Loneliness? Fear of what my future might be?

In Your Workbook or *Courage and Grace Freedom Journal*, Answer the Following:

Why have I wept?

What have I done to move forward and heal?

Step Two

Today I Raged, and that's Okay

    Be honest and write down all the reasons you were raging. Express the why followed with what steps you are taking to move forward and let go of the anger. Why exactly are you angry? Feeling humiliated? Angry with yourself? Or with him? Angry you had to give up your home?

In Your Workbook or *Courage and Grace Freedom Journal,* Answer the Following:

Why have I Raged?

What have I done to move forward & heal?

Breathing Exercises

To Be Done Before Writing or Reconnecting

When I'm suffering from self-doubt or tonnes of negative self-talk is creeping in and making me feel unworthy or inadequate, I stop what I'm working on and disconnect all of my electronic devices so I can sit quietly without interruption or distraction. Then I close my eyes and breathe in relaxation and breathe out negativity; breathe in confidence and breathe out self-doubt. I'll breathe for 8 or 10 times, nice deep, soothing breaths.

Then I begin the magic of visualisation. I see my goal, where I want to be, and what I'll be feeling when I get there. I can hear all the good things people have to say, I see myself happy and my clients smiling, I see and feel how proud I am of myself, and how comfortable I am with my voice and body. It works like a charm.

Begin with the Following Pattern:

Breathe in through your nose...
    and out through your mouth
Breathe in goodness...
    breathe out negativity
Breathe in peace...
    breathe out stress
Breathe in happiness...
    breathe out sorrow

The process of filling your lungs with good feelings and emptying them of negative feelings is cleansing. You will feel quiet and peaceful. It promotes a clarity of thought and places you in a positive, creative space.

I love breathing, meditating, and visualising and this is one of my favourite guided breathing and calming exercises. It is soothing, calming, and peaceful. After you listen, you'll be feeling very relaxed and ready to write and reconnect with your authentic desires and goals.

Breathing for Calmness and Clarity Meditation

http://www.susanball.ca/breathing-relaxation-meditations/

DISCONNECTING AND RECONNECTING WITH SMALL JOYFUL THINGS

You have been through the fires of hell, and to survive, you lost touch with the small joyful things that used to make you smile and feel happy. Just happy.

Disconnect...

Turn off all your devices—cell phone, computer, tablets, TV. There is no space for cheating—disconnect from all electronic devices!

Reconnect with Small Joyful Things

STEP ONE: When you were little, what did you want to be when you grew up? We all had a dream, but people get sidetracked from their dreams by status, money, responsibility, and life.

Answer the following questions in your Workbook or Freedom Journal:

As a child, what did you want to be?

As a child, what made you laugh?

STEP TWO: Remembering your childhood dreams can help you reconnect with the real you and lead you to joy as an adult. Discovering what you enjoy along with activities that help you laugh, will change your mood + your perception.

In Your Workbook or *Courage and Grace Freedom Journal*, Answer the Following:

As an Adult, What Activities Do You Enjoy?

STEP THREE: Pick a day each week and block off time just for you. This is non-negotiable. This is your special time. It's a date with you to reconnect with your small joyful things.

Answer the following in your Workbook:

This Week, To Bring Me Joy, I Will?

Hold this time for you. No excuses. Remember you teach others how to treat you by your example. If you're willing to break your own dates, others will leave you behind as well.

Do something you enjoy. Something to bring you a moment of happiness and fulfilment.

You deserve it!

WRITING FROM THE HEART

Writing Journal Prompts

Writing is healing. It allows you to express gratitude, fear, success, and challenges. Writing also allows you to connect with a part of your mind, the creative, planning part, not easily reached with speaking.

Take time to create a beautiful Journal. Make it your own. Add photos, feathers, beads or any item that makes you smile. On the inside front cover, make it your own by writing your name in big, bold letters.

When You Open Your Journal, At the Top of Each Page, Write:

- *Today, I forgive myself for any mistakes I may make*
- *I am enough*
- *Every day, in every way, I'm getting better and better*

Journal prompts open our minds and our thinking. I know when I first started journaling, I purchased a book with daily writing prompts. They were helpful in getting my creative juices flowing and encouraging me to write freely about a variety of topics. Prompts, create freestyle writing, and that can lead to amazing self-discoveries.

Here Are Three of My Favourite Prompts:

What Can I Create Today?

What Did I Learn I Can Do Today?

What Did I Give Today?

Courage and Grace

Appendix B

THE 7 WARNING SIGNS OF A MEAN-SPIRITED DICK

The signs are always right in front of us. Several personal factors, especially low self-worth contribute to our acceptance of abuse in relationships. Even the strongest amongst us can be worn down in time with sweet words, undying adoration and passion, and the feeling we will be loved and cherished.

When I met my handsome abuser, I did not know how to drive. I lived in a big city with great public transit and didn't see the need for all the expense associated with having a car. All my life I had dreamed of owning a Jeep Wrangler. Driving without doors or a roof – it exemplified the ultimate freedom to me. *Odd dream for a girl who couldn't drive.* On a beautiful sunny day, my love drove up in a bright cherry-red Jeep Wrangler and told me he had bought it for me. Of course, I gushed and jumped for joy and felt so lucky. He had listened to my dreams and acted upon them!

Here's the catch. As we were driving around and I was feeling fabulous, I said that it was time for me to learn to drive. I had my dream vehicle, now I needed to drive it. He laughed so hard, he had to pull over to the side of the road. He said I was too clumsy and uncoordinated to drive a vehicle and he would never let me drive the Jeep or even practice in it. At that moment, he delivered the typical give a little – take more pattern of emotional abuse. I had my Jeep, but it was a carrot he dangled in front of me.

I wish I'd learned the 7 Warning Signs as a young woman and given them my full attention. With knowledge of these signs and a little common sense, I would have found the power to say, "There is no way in hell that I will allow someone to treat me like a piece of crap!"

When we lack self-love and self-worth, we stifle our real authentic voice and don't stand up for ourselves. The best time to escape an abusive relationship is before it starts but without the knowledge, experience, and healthy self-worth, we are all susceptible to this trap. Manipulative men instinctively know our dreams and offer them up on a silver platter.

That's how I got caught and trapped. Because of child abandonment issues, my self-love was so low that hearing him say, "I want to spend my every waking moment with you," was wonderful. I fell fully into his trap. If I'd had the self-love I do now, I would have used my voice and said, "That's sweet, but I love my time alone and with my other friends. I don't need anyone to consume my every waking moment."

The 7 Signs He's Going to be a Mean-Spirited Dick

If you recognise any of these signs, run the other way. Do not excuse him or think it's sweet or cute. Run!

1. **Love Bombs**– the Love word gets tossed out the second time you're together. He loves you and couldn't imagine life without you. It is manipulation. Run as fast as you can! If he's talking about it already, that's not love.
2. **Provider** – all he wants to do is look after you and your kids. "Now that I've met you, baby, that's all I live for." Do you need someone to look after you? And what does he mean when he says, "look after you?"
3. **Emotional Extortion** because he's going to spend a day, night, or an hour without you. This is classic manipulation to make you feel guilt and shame. You know you want to go out with your friends or stay home alone or visit your mom – Do That! Do not give into his crying for your attention. Live your life and keep it separate.
4. **Isolation**: He starts by telling you that others are deceiving and manipulating you and you want to avoid them. This is the classic pot calling the kettle black situation. Let's call it the Reversal

5. ***Manipulation***: You will often hear him use your own argument against you or your friends. If you've known your friends since kindergarten and you feel comfortable telling them your deepest, darkest secrets, keep doing it because you know your friends best. He does not.

6. ***Anticipatory Fear***: You feel on edge when it's time to see him, you don't know why but you feel like something is going to happen that is not good. In the dating stage, this is often expressed as a fear of enduring his disappointment or disapproval.

7. ***Impossible Expectations***: Do you wonder if you can meet his expectations? Especially the silent, unspoken ones? He wants you to dress a certain way or behave a certain way that is not you. Does he pick out what you wear or show you pictures of clothes or beautiful women on the Internet and ask you to dress or look like them? Does he tell you how to behave when you're out with his family or friends? Do you even know what he expects from you?

8. **SEX**. *He will demand, take, coerce, or manipulate you. You find yourself having sex because you felt you had no choice. You didn't, and you're correct. That is not love or respect. It is unhealthy. Years and years ago, the Royal Army separated the charge of sexual assault into two divisions: FUCK and RAPE. The lesser crime, Forced Use of Carnal Knowledge, was most often applied if the victim was a woman of lower social ranking. If he wants and takes Sex and you give in, you are being FUCKed! If you do not give consent, it's Rape, plan and simple.*

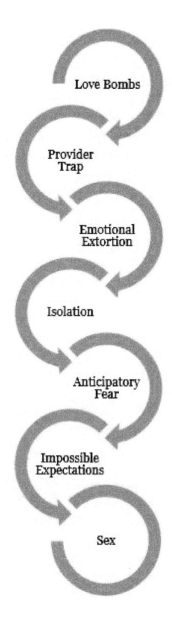

The 7 Signs He's Going to be a Mean-Spirited Dick details the Decent into Abuse

Consider this the slippery-slope. Once you start your descent, it becomes more and more difficult to pull yourself up and clear of your abuser. I invite you to share this with every woman you know, especially teenage girls just starting to date. Memorise each step. Learning to spot the Mean Spirited Dick at a distance is your best defence. And whatever you do, don't fall into the trap of thinking this one, or this time is different. If he's tossing the Love Bomp or dangling the Provider Trap, there is no question He's A Mean Spirited Dick.

Appendix C

BREATHING EXERCISES AND SELF-GUIDED MEDITATION

Taking a deep breath and letting it out slowly will reset your thinking, ease your tension and improve your outlook.

A trip to the beach to relax, enjoy the sun, water, relaxation and cooling breeze, is a great way to unwind at the end of the day or when you're feeling overwhelmed.

Visit the link below to access:
Breathing Relaxation Meditations

http://www.susanball.ca/breathing-relaxation-meditations/

Last Thoughts...

Congratulations! You have worked hard, and I'm so proud of you for liberating your Blissful Thriver.

You are worthy of all that you dream of. You are capable of creating a life filled with happiness, peace, joy, love, and passion. There is nothing holding you back. Those old stories have no power over you, and the new ones are big, bold and juicy!

You are on fire, and you have the momentum to make your goals your reality. Success comes in all sizes – celebrate them all with a big bang.

I believe in you, and I want to hear your Broken to Blissful Story of Success. Send your story to susan@susanball.ca, and I will reply personally.

Reviews are always welcome and appreciated. Leave one on Amazon or write to me personally! Amazon:

https://www.amazon.com/Susan-Ball/e/B01MF5NKNC/

How to Contact Susan

Online at www.susanball.ca

By email at susan@susanball.ca

Facebook: Broken to Blissful Group

https://www.facebook.com/groups/brokentoblissful/

Twitter: https://twitter.com/lifecoachsusanb

I Invite You to Reserve Your VIP Session With Me:

http://www.susanball.ca/be-my-v-i-p/

NOTES